D1622204

THE RETURN OF MOTHER GOD

The Feminine Essence of Our Creator

Tony Scazzero

Dedicated to Father and Mother God

Also by Tony Scazzero

Drink Your Own Water

All About the Spirit World

Who Is Mother God?

Our Mother and Father God

Power Animals and Their Symbolism

The Virtues of Women

The author wishes to thank the creators of all copyrighted material used and quoted in this book, all of which has been duly acknowledged in the reference notes. The author releases this book under the Fair Use clause of the 1976 US Copyright. Every effort has been made to locate and acquire permissions from each source quoted. If any persons mentioned do not wish to be included in this book, they are encouraged to notify the publisher and we will have their quotes cheerfully removed.

Special gratitude to medium C.K. for channeling Mother God's messages.

Cover artwork by Gene Garbowski (genegarbowski@yahoo.com)

Table of Contents

Preface

Tony Scazzero is profoundly devoted to Mother God. His extensively researched *The Return of Mother God* is more than timely as we usher in the Age of Aquarius which is truly the age of the Divine Mother.

All are called to come to know Mother God intimately during these times of great change. Whether she is called the Divine Feminine, Great Mother, or another name, the Goddess is inviting us back to her supreme love to bring balance and healing into our troubled world.

For too many centuries, Mother God was rarely mentioned and the toll of patriarchal ways on women and the Earth has been more than harsh. For too long women experience needless suffering and were even killed because of their healing gifts and connection to the Divine Mother. Global devastation of ecosystems and climate changes now speak to the terribly unwise ways civilization has forgotten to revere our Mother Earth.

As women have begun to step into their personal power and claim positions of leadership in society, there is the growing recognition that our religious systems have denied the awareness of the feminine aspect within Creation. In seeking balance and rights as equal partners to men, it is important that women look to the spiritual realms as well for that sacred balance.

For men, embracing Mother God is a path of knowing divine compassion and comfort that can restore peace within their hearts and also within the world. We are all children of Mother God and Father God.

Mystics who can hear the cry of our Earth Mother share her call to remember her and sacredly reconnect with her. Just as Mother God is a universal force of Divine Energy, we are blessed with a Planetary Caretaker who is sacred and feminine in energy. She too is yearning for us to shift into wiser ways in alignment with her.

It is time for us to welcome Mother God into our hearts and minds, so that we can move forward in the evolution of our higher consciousness on Earth. We need to wake up and step into full maturity as spiritual beings, miraculously gifted with sacred physical bodies lent to us by Earth Mother in this journey. The love of the Mother awaits us and what a glorious love it is! Once Mother touches your heart, your life will know more joy and comfort than you ever thought possible.

~ Mare Cromwell, author of *The Great Mother Bible*

Award Winning and Amazon bestselling Author, Nature Mystic, Empathic Intuitive Healer & International Speaker. http://www.marecromwell.com

Introduction

"You'll spend your whole life looking for God and not finding Her. Because you're looking for *Him*."[1]
Neale Donald Walsch

In a world of cover-ups and conspiracies, one has to wonder if everything is being disclosed about the divinity of God. Is it possible that "religions" have not been totally transparent? Is it possible that some things or someone have been overlooked, disregarded, or suppressed? In particular, is there a reason why only a masculine God is spoken about in the major faith traditions? If our Father is in heaven, where is our Mother? Has She been forgotten, hidden, or perhaps ignored? Has Her abandonment caused our global family to languish without a Divine Mother, thereby permitting the world's problems to increase? In spite of these possibilities, and unknown to most people, She is now returning. Author Jean Shinoda Bolen, MD, who has been following this trend for years, observes, "The Sacred Feminine is coming back, mostly through women, but also men who have dreams of numinous goddess figures or who follow their intuition and instinct."[2] There is ample evidence that this change in consciousness concerning the return of the Divine Mother God is not a fluke, nor a flash in the pan. Here is a glimpse of the future and we need to take heed. Humanity has to be transformed to find it's original purpose. There is a universal sense that "something" is missing. Indeed, there is no true joy in having only a masculine Divine Parent. The purpose of this book is to shed light on this point.

Recent studies have shown that in many early civilizations, worship of female deities pervaded most cultures. Despite that, some Eastern religions with their goddesses are dismissed as pagan or superstitious belief systems. Although men tend to dismiss female gods or goddesses, the further back one looks into our human past, the more the evidence there is of belief in goddesses alongside of the gods. As Vajra Ma says, "In the ancient Indian tradition of the Divine Mother, Shakti is the Feminine power. It is the oldest spiritual lineage on Earth, humanity's more than 200,000 years of universal reference for the source of life: The Great Cosmic Mother."[3] It would seem, at least from a pre-Vedic perspective, it is Her womb from which humanity, at the beginning of time, was birthed. Tricia McCannon, in her recent book, *Return of the Divine Sophia,* envisions it as follows:

> Honoring the Goddess was the first theology of our ancestors. They believed that the creator of the universe is female, but in the last few thousand years, people have forgotten who She is, so now the world has fallen out of balance. When we remember Her, we restore balance to the world.[4]

In monotheistic religions, a male God favors men and gives men dominion over women, children, and all living things. However, according to mythology and a good deal of archeology, before there was a God, there was a Goddess. The Bible contains little or no information about this divine feminine nature, even though it does say that the first man and woman were made in the image of God. Somehow, the Divine Feminine as a divine maternal force was suppressed and driven underground, into the collective unconscious. Author Paul R. Smith, who penned the book, *Is It Okay to Call God "Mother"?* believes that our society is somewhat molded and directed by the way we perceive the divine power. He writes:

> Our image of God has vast social ramifications. If God, who is creative, all-knowing, powerful, and dominant is characterized as male, then male must be more like God than female. Males must therefore be strong, creative, all-knowing, powerful, and dominant. The implication is that females must be the opposite – weak, uncreative, ignorant, powerless, and submissive.[5]

Eliminating the femininity and promoting the masculinity of God has done not only women but humanity as a whole a great disservice. It has negated the important positions of women in the home, the society, and the world. Although women have virtues and strengths that are different from those of men, they both have complementary God-given abilities. Acknowledging the feminine nature of God would naturally give women complementary equal value with men in God's original design. Rev. Jann Aldredge-Clanton states it emphatically, "Understanding the Divine as feminine will help society realize that women and men are equal and need to be treated equally in all aspects of life."[6] Why shouldn't women be allowed their divine rights as sparks from that divine flame? Alix Pirani believes that such a change in society would initiate a healing for the entire planet and all its inhabitants. In *The Absent Mother* she explains it this way:

> To heal and revive our world and all the people in it, we need to look again at the older religious traditions that sought and followed a female God, or within God, or aspect of God. The Divine She, the Mother Earth and Queen of Heaven, the She of the underworld, all

express a concept that has been swept from the patriarchal thought and tradition.[7]

When we exclude the feminine side of God, disastrous changes occur worldwide. Relations between men and women are set in a mode that oppresses both women and nature. Reconciling the past with an authentic respect for the feminine viewpoint would rectify this. If truth be told, the feminine aspect of God's nature has long been obscured and hidden in the patriarchal traditions of Judaism and Christianity. In *A Chariot Drawn by Lions,* Asphodel P. Long expresses the concerns of many, that changes must be made in society if we are to survive, and that emphasizing the divine feminine could be the key. She writes, "Today, reclaiming Wisdom, seeking Her, rejoicing in Her and understanding Her ways, is one way in which changes can be made that must come about if not only in relationships in society but also if the world itself is to be renewed safely and harmoniously."[8]

If this resurrection of the Goddess in theology is so important to human survival, why is it so difficult for nations and religions to accept the presence of the Divine Feminine? Some religious persons, especially those who have been traumatized in the name of religion, may have difficulty seeing the world as other than black and white. They think that the one God must be *either* male *or* female. But to embrace the Great Mother does not mean we turn our back on the Divine Father. They are two aspects of the same entity. In fact, in its most transcendental aspects, God would logically be above gender, and as the Creator of both male and female, possessing aspects of both. Most historians of the Bible would agree that the Holy Spirit (Shekinah in the Old Testament) is, or at least reflects, that feminine side. As

Patricia Taylor writes in her book, *The Holy Spirit, the Feminine Nature of God:*

> Having a more truthful image of God would open the spirits of people to receive the one true God. As this truth changes the status and well-being of women around the world, it will also improve the condition of our hurting families.[9]

By "the one true God," Taylor is referring here to One with both feminine and masculine aspects, turning on its head the commonplace image of the old man with the beard, which Abrahamic fundamentalists call "the one true God." She conveys the feeling that this image of God is an untruthful one, which implies that at least certain religious leaders should know better but don't confess. Throughout the world, we are currently witnessing a huge resurgence of feminine influence. If we look around, there are more than a few feminine ideas and breakthroughs occurring. A distinctive mystical influence is developing, revolutionizing the way humanity thinks about women. What is behind this profound change in the collective consciousness about women? Andrew Harvey, Oxford-educated author of thirty books and founder of "Sacred Activism," sees it as a basic question of balance. In *The Divine Feminine*, he writes, "To counterbalance the existing situation that has one-sided emphasis, the image of the Divine Feminine, together with the mythological tradition that belongs to it, is returning to consciousness."[10] Harvey is not banning any mention of a male God, he is simply urging us to think bigger, more inclusively.

Jennifer Woolger goes to the mythological core of the situation, reminding us that the attributes that world mythology grants to the feminine are ones we cannot possibly exist without. In the classic *The Goddess Within,* she argues:

> All creative and inspiration thinking, all nurturing, mothering and gestating, all passion, desire and sexuality, all urges toward connectedness, social cohesion, union and communion, all merging and fusion as well as impulses to absorb, to destroy, to reproduce, and to replicate belong to the universal archetype of the feminine.[11]

Realigning ourselves with sacred principles of gender harmony is crucial for our world to heal. Many feel an unpleasant stress in their daily lives because of an imbalance on the spiritual level. Ecological crises that trigger earthquakes, volcanoes, tidal waves, tornadoes, and other natural catastrophes are visible symptoms of the world's imbalances. Moreover, inequalities and iniquities in the world attest to the substantial shortcomings of modern civilization's knowledge. Until the existing state of affairs between men and women attains an equal balance, a harmonious culture will stay a daydream. Only the restoration of feminine divinity, long overdue, can wake up humanity which is in desperate need of revitalization. Author Tricia McCannon suggests we do not need to invent new and complex solutions to the vast and entangled problems of society; we merely need to go back to our roots as a species, one that possessed answers about our relationship with the Divine Mother from the beginning of time. In *The Return of the Divine Sophia,* she writes, "The mysteries of the past hold keys to recovering this inner balance that can help us to transform the world."[12] That is not to suggest that these problems are minor or can be easily brushed aside.

The world is overdue for a spiritual upgrade, as our beliefs about God and life are no longer justifiable. We find ourselves on a planet rife with suffering and loneliness, and the political, economic, social, and religious systems are largely to blame, or at least insufficiently capable of dealing with them.[13]

At this critical junction, the integration of feminine and masculine principles can bring new hope and purpose. Slowly but surely, a renewed understanding of the gender-balanced duality of the Godhead is emerging. This 'reunited' Supreme Being validates two aspects of consciousness to empower both men and women. Yet, the revival or return of the Divine Feminine is not a new idea. What's more, the re-emergence of the Divine Feminine has been anticipated in many spiritual messages and prophecies. In 1993, like a voice in the wilderness, visionary Christian Paul R. Smith told us: "Until there is peace between male and female in our image of God, there will be no peace between male and female."[14] His work now reaches multitudes but the distance between men and women in relationships is still a major theme in literature. Existing patriarchal habits and traditions, including language customs, block a wholesome attitude toward life. Today's troubling issues could find promising and viable answers through a Divine Feminine approach, especially in delicate matters involving the genders. With the divine as the standard bearer, it will be natural to find the way so that things will get back on the right track.

Author Asphodel Long thinks that names have power, and believes that, "The naming of God as female, or at least having the female named as an aspect of God, has enormous consequences, not the least is our attitude to the world itself."[15] Long would agree that we have suffered many unnecessary misfortunes since Mother

God was replaced and eradicated from Scriptures and history books. One horrific consequence of leaving Mother God out of life's choices may have been the loss of a harmonious and peaceful world, especially in the realm of relationships. Could it be that there's something in the masculine image of God alone that actually contributes to the problems and prevents us from finding the solutions we so desperately need? Perhaps it is time we take into consideration the female, mothering aspect of God's nature.

Why is it so difficult to admit that the patriarchal view of God may be wrong? God's relating to humanity has been prejudiced by Judeo-Christian ways that follow the masculine perception. It is not adequate and it has not brought the not ideal. Why has civilization chosen that perspective? In the past, people saw the divine as a female because it was naturally deduced that the ability to produce and nurture life began from a mother. As far back as ancient times, women and feminine principles were highly esteemed. For many women, as well as men, the image of God never lacked a female aspect. The Divine Feminine has always been the model for all women. According to Joy F. Reichard, it will be so again. "Today there is a growing movement that honors the Divine Feminine and many are reclaiming the goddess as a symbol of empowerment for women."[16] It is a prospect that She and millions of others look forward to with great hope.

What would happen if everyone imagined God as female, as a mother? How would it affect our relationships with each other and the Earth? Would atrocities such as war and abject poverty be allowed to exist? Would the pursuit of money, power, and position be the primary motivations of the day? Would so much mental and emotional sickness be allowed to continue and grow? Thinking people, the world over, should address these challenging questions. Incredibly, virtuous women, who have been held back, embody humanity's greatest resource to resolve the world's troubles. A woman of humble foresight, Vajra Ma, said in 2013, "The resurgence of the Feminine Power will provide the power we need to pierce the demons of the modern era, spiritual ignorance, rapacious greed and violence."[17] This is wisdom that speaks to our hearts. Carole Schaefer, in her book *Grandmothers Counsel the World,* observed:

> In today's world the power of the feminine – the most potent, loving, and creative of forces on Earth – is severely suppressed, and if not again honored, the imbalance of male and female energies could cause the destruction of humanity, if not the Earth Herself.[18]

The benefits of hailing a Divine Feminine in these times are not just a matter of damage control. Such a shift should well unleash powerful creative and healing forces in both men and women. Modern women are getting in touch with their innate spiritual femininity, something that was so often overlooked in past decades. Once a woman identifies with her intrinsic goddess-like nature, she will be inspired to realize her innate, creative potential. There are symbols of powerful female deities all over the world that provide female-affirming archetypes for women to imitate. Once women discover and accept the Divine Feminine as the origin of all that is beneficial, they will really feel liberated because they will have discovered the highest exemplar of women's full potential. Without Mother God, girls and women have no Sacred Feminine role model they can emulate or identify with. Joy F. Reichard presents a simple and credible solution when she writes, "Identifying with the Sacred Feminine is a means for a woman to feel the divine within so she can more readily embrace her own qualities of strength, beauty, and power."[19]

What does this Divine Feminine look like? She has taken many forms, such as the Goddess Sophia, a goddess of wisdom, who appears in Western civilization in many roles. In *Return of the Divine Sophia,* Tricia McCannon writes:

> The goddess has reappeared in different times and places. As the powers of the goddesses waned, so did the rights of women. By worshiping the Father principle alone, and suppressing or belittling the feminine, we have done serious damage to our individual and collective health."[20]

In a nutshell, McCannon says that the neglect and removal of the Divine Feminine has created a massive imbalance in the world, resulting in the internal and external polarization between men and women. The failure of existing theologies to integrate Mother and Father God into their thinking has had a resounding impact upon the whole world. Without clear images of how the gender-balanced divine is reflected in their lives, human beings cannot advance and achieve excellence in their lives. What's more, humanity has currently reached an impasse, even a breaking point, in resolving many of its crises. However, there are signs of hope, signs that we are already entering a new cycle of time where the rise of the feminine will be evident to all. Caitlin Matthews, in her book *Sophia,* writes: "We have entered into an era when hidden mysteries are to take their proper and acknowledged place, in order that the regenerative feminine can help restore the Earth."[21] Sylvia Brown speaks of the stirring that the Divine Feminine will bring to life in the near future:

> She has been put to sleep for many years, although She has always been walking through the Earth. But once She has been awakened – as She was by the Gnostic movement – people began to bring Her more to life, so to speak, in their world. Then She had absolute power to come in.[22]

Appreciating how women are made in God's image from Mother God can alter society's perspectives significantly. At any rate, a quiet advocacy for innate human freedoms has been developing for years. Without question, a growing number of people from an assortment of countries understand that the Divine Feminine is vital for gender equality and justice. Replacing the existing consciousness utilizing God's masculine and feminine traits would create a more nurturing and wholesome energy. Again, Paul R. Smith sees this theological problem at the root of many relationship—and therefore family—problems. He writes, "Underlying the challenge of how men and women are to relate is the image of God."[23] What he is saying is that when you have an image of God that is only male, and this is accepted, it is difficult for both men and women to stand on equal footing and relate to each other as equals.

Call it a transcendent state of awareness, a higher consciousness, or just virtue, but women have something extraordinary that men are lacking and unable to get by without. Women naturally appreciate relationships more than spreadsheets. They have an innate understanding of how to interpret situations in order to see what the future will hold. Women value feelings, imagination, and understanding more than external expertise, logic, or materiality. They perceive the bigger picture, carry a more holistic, awareness, and command a mystic intuition as their birthright. Primarily, women appreciate process as much as the end result. Perhaps it is for this reason, if not others, that Vajra Ma was correct when she stated, "Only Woman can bring humanity back into right relationship."[24] At the very least, women will insist we focus as much on the process as on the goal, and this will prevent us from repeating many of our recent mistakes as a species.

Describing the Spirit of God is not easy, even with extensive academic, theological, or philosophical acumen. Explanations, depictions, and interpretations of God vary far and wide. The question of comprehending the Godhead is so challenging that most people leave it to faith or just leave it alone. Nevertheless, due to present-day circumstances, it is critical at this point in time to reexamine our image of God. The positive effect an even slight enhancement in our understanding of the Godhead cannot be overstated. Tricia McCannon finds an expression of the polarization that has created a battle of the divine sexes in the field of psychology. She writes, "Jungian psychologists say that in creating this extreme polarization between a negative, condemning, judgmental God and a banished, loving mother, we have actually denied ourselves a healthy spiritual life."[25] In addition, she states:

> The spirit of the Divine Feminine has been dishonored, manipulated, misrepresented, and suppressed, and it is only now, in this time, in this century, that our civilization is beginning to question what exactly has thrown us out of balance. Restoring the feminine to its rightful place in partnership with the masculine, with both as true equals, is the most important step we can

take today if we are ever to claim our place as caretakers of this planet and take our next step as enlightened human beings.[26]

Logic tells us that if there is a God the Father, there also must be a God the Mother. Universal recognition of the rationality behind a gender-balanced Godhead could become the foundation for world harmony and peace. Yet, somehow we have forgotten who our Mother is even though there is more than ample evidence of Her spirit as a living being. But there is much more to the Divine Mother than the logic of Her existence. In fact, rarely has human culture existed, until the modern era, that has failed to recognize the importance of the feminine aspect of the Creator. Although constantly negated in Western religion, She has the power and authority to change deeply held patriarchal attitudes and beliefs. The future will be redesigned when women have the all the necessary tools. Then they will be empowered to make even more contributions to the world. In fact, the modern increase of women's ability to facilitate change, together with the re-emergence of the Divine Feminine, is earth-shattering. This extraordinary return of Mother God will have far-reaching implications that will bring civilization to an entirely new level both spiritually and physically. Without a doubt, once humanity becomes aware of this higher viewpoint, the ideal world will begin to take shape. As I have stated in *Our Mother and Father God*, "Mother and Father God, the source of beauty, truth and goodness, are the role models for the gender-balanced principles and values needed to solve the world's problems."[27]

Chapter 1
Goddesses Past

The Goddess belief is uniquely both ancient and modern. The authenticity and symbolism of the Goddess has been humanity's most persistent devotion since the foundation of the world. In many parts of the world, we can still observe the widespread worship of a female Goddess. This type of worship has been around for thousands of years and has the longest history of all the world's religions. It has played a widespread and significant role in most cultures and civilizations. "The Goddess, as Mother Earth, has been considered supreme in many ancient traditions."[28] McCannon stresses exactly how ancient this view really is. In *Return of the Divine Sophia*, she traces it back more than two hundred millennia.

> God was considered Female for at least the first 200,000 years of human life on earth! And, in fact, the only image of the Creator ever painted on rock, carved in stone or sculpted in clay for a period of about 30,000 years was that of the Divine Mother. While this statement seems almost incomprehensible to those of us raised in conventional contemporary societies, once we examine the anthropological evidence it becomes an indisputable truth.[29]

Although locked away for the last few thousand years in the Western world, the Goddess has awakened periodically to let Herself be known. The Divine Feminine image of the universal Mother has unceasingly been the heart and soul of humanity. In fact, the Great Mother archetype continues to manifest in different ways across different cultures. For this reason, it holds the promise to reinvigorate society, and women in particular, like nothing else. Now is the time to reexamine the past and reclaim our full humanity with the Divine Feminine. Once we recognize and accept our spiritual history, it will be easy to re-establish the balance of masculinity and femininity in the world. If Earth truly is our "mother," this shift in religious terminology towards the feminine could lead to new breakthroughs in environmental science as well. Joy Reichard puts it this way, "Understanding our ancient ancestors' appreciation and connection to the natural world will strengthen our own connection to the Earth, the Great Mother."[30] Author Anne Baring goes one step further and not only acknowledges the ancient recognition by humanity of the Great Mother, as seen through early drawings and carvings, but at the same time humanity's early realization of itself as a child of Nature. If we are to move towards reinstating the Earth as our Mother, we might have to rediscover our lost innocence as Her children as well. Baring remarks:

> Looking back so many thousands of years later at the earliest archeological figures, it seems as if humanity's first image of life was the Mother. This must go back to a time when human beings experienced themselves as the children of Nature, in relationship with all things, part of the whole.[31]

In the distant past, the Goddess and the God were apparently worshiped as both the creator and the destroyer of life. One thing is for certain, throughout the long journey of human life on earth, there has never been a time or place that did not include the female aspect of God—at least until recently; the last few seconds of humanity's day in the sun. Greek goddesses are images of women that have lived in the human imagination for over three thousand years. Today the Goddess still exists, if only as an archetype in the collective unconscious and will be impossible to erase, no matter how deeply we slip into denial. There will always be those who celebrate Her presence. "Cultures throughout the world, including Hinduism, Native American traditions, and African religions, each pay homage to the Divine Feminine.[32] Joy Reichard notes that women in this age of the Internet can, for perhaps the first time in history, access information about goddesses from all over the world, and perhaps find strength in them. In *Celebrate the Divine Feminine,* she comments:

> A woman in need of healing might reach out to Kuan Yin, Mother Mary, or Our Lady of Guadalupe – all Divine Feminine archetypes of compassion and mercy whose consoling presence provides comfort and support during the darkest hour. If in need of courage a woman might call upon Kali, who fearlessly fights demons. If it's wisdom and strategic thinking that's needed a woman might call upon Artemis the Huntress, or Athena, Goddess of Wisdom.[33]

The primary feature that ancient cultures had in common was their awareness and worship of the divine Goddess. She was known by many names in many cultures and was responsible for the fertility and destructiveness of nature. Her grandeur was captured in pottery, jewelry, paintings, and statues across large portions of Greece, Italy, Africa, Iraq, and Egypt. No matter how it was expressed, the overshadowing concept was that of a mother. Author Susanne Schaup sees the Mother as a unifying symbol for early cultures. She writes, "In the center of early human culture stood the Great Goddess or Mother Goddess as a divine symbol of life and of the unity of humankind and nature."[34] There are many types of goddesses but the maternal seems to be the most persistent of all.

There is no doubt that, throughout the world, people have felt the need to represent the Goddess with a maternal image, whether it be part of an Earth Mother, a Virgin Mother, or some similar spiritual nature. The very fact that pre-Christian religions worshiped a Mother Goddess made the transition from one ideology to another easy; the ritual remained the same.[35]

The scope and significance of the reverence paid to the Goddess over twenty-five thousand years ago cuts across many national boundaries and over vast expanses of the sea. It would take an encyclopedia of information to express the longevity and widespread influence the Mother Goddess had. The Goddess was known in almost every area of the Near and Middle East. In fact, worship of the female deity survived into the classical periods of Greece and Rome. Her influence was immense. She was not suppressed until the time of the Christian emperors of Rome and Byzantium, who closed down the last Goddess temples in the fifth century. Merlin Stone's book *When God Was a Woman,* caused quite a stir when it was released in 1976. In its controversial pages she emphasized times and places where the worship of the Divine Feminine was not only acceptable but also the dominant paradigm. "The archeological artifacts suggest that in all the Neolithic and early Chalcolithic societies the Divine Ancestress, generally referred to by most writers as the Mother Goddess, was revered as the supreme deity."[36] What is implied here is that the newer patriarchal religions with their male Supreme Being were on a collision course with the older beliefs. Asphodel Long spells out the conflict more directly:

A very long-lived veneration, born in the earliest stages of human history and classified as one of the major religions of the Hellenistic world, was that of the Great

Mother. She existed as a goddess to be worshipped with splendor and awe well into late Roman times and challenged the young and expanding Christianity of that era.[37]

The introduction of the worship of the Goddess Isis to Greece and Rome coincided with the greater emancipation of women in what had become rigidly patriarchal cultures. The goddesses represented freedom from oppression and allowed women to exercise a unique power and diversity of behavior. In a number of societies where the Mother Goddess was revered, women were evidently highly valued. In fact, women in ancient Egypt enjoyed a high status in society, reflecting the sovereignty of Isis in the spiritual realm. Merlin Stone, ever conscious of the sexual politics of history, wrote, "Wherever they worshipped a Goddess, women held a high status, or because women held a high status, therefore a Goddess was worshipped."[38] It was a synchronicity that went beyond chance. It forces us to acknowledge the political impact of theology. Author Carol Christ proclaims:

> The rediscovery of the Goddess has provoked a reconsideration of the roles of women and goddesses in the origin and history of religion. Based on several decades of research, a new interpretative framework draws together archeological, historical, and anthropological evidence and theory. In it, both women and goddesses play important roles in human history.[39]

Not only are we urged to acknowledge the importance of the Goddess in early human history, but the importance of women living in that era as well. Many cultures, including those of Egypt, Greece, and Rome, shared different stories about the Goddess, which they personified with individual names. By studying the myths and archeology of the Goddess from around the world we can enlarge our understanding of this powerful feminine figure that was the sustainer of life. She was imagined as earth and all parts of nature. Moreover, She was seen in everything, both visible and invisible. Author M. J. Labadie urges us to see beyond any one form the Goddess may take historically, but perceive the oneness behind all Her incarnations. She maintains, "As we consider the Goddess it is necessary to realize that no matter which of Her aspects is told about in the myths – we are really talking about the One Goddess."[40] Simone de Beauvoir states it poetically:

> In primitive times, a veritable reign of women existed based on the Great Goddess or Great Mother statues that have been excavated. She is the queen of heaven, yet the dove is Her symbol. She can be seen in mountains, woods, the sea, and springs. She creates life everywhere.[41]

All the goddesses transmitted the feeling that they could be appealed to for help, guidance, and inspiration. Believers often experienced a wellspring of love. When speaking with the Goddess, there was no separation between spiritual and physical, imagination and reality. Andrew Harvey, in *The Divine Feminine,* acknowledges that, "The Great Mother was the nurturing and regenerating power that sustained all creation. She was the water of life on which people depended for food, the terror of the raging storm, the dew-bringing moonlight, the warmth of the Sun that ripened the wheat and the barley. She was life and death."[42] In *Goddesses in Every Woman,* which was released in 1984, Jean Shinoda Bolen implied that knowledge of the various goddesses and their stories grants women permission to emulate them, even though conventional society would never allow women this kind of spiritual and creative power. Bolen wrote:

> It is possible to invoke a goddess by consciously making effort to see, feel, or sense Her presence – to bring Her into focus through the imagination – and then ask for Her particular strength. When goddesses are seen as patterns of normal feminine behavior, a woman can be true to her feminine self by resembling a particular Greek goddess.[43]

One way or another, the goddesses and their supporters have survived throughout Western civilization. Although patriarchal leaders tried to minimize Her standing and stature, they could not totally disregard each person's affection for different Goddess personifications. She was even retained by the war-loving Greeks, although Her division into the separate roles of the different goddesses left Her weakened and one-sided in Her functions and powers. Asphodel Long, author of *In a Chariot Drawn by Lions,* traces the Divine Feminine's long descent into obscurity and submission in Western civilization. She writes, "In the cultures before Christianity, the idea of the divine as female was never totally lost. It was obscured in Judaism and moved underground into the Shekinah. In Christianity, the notion of female wisdom was subsumed into Jesus Christ, subsequently into the third person of the Trinity, the Holy Spirit, and eventually into Mother Church."[44] But McCannon reminds us that even at the height of the patriarchy, the Goddess was still acknowledged in all Her forms as Queen of Heaven, a term we find in *The Book of Inanna,* in reference to the all-powerful Sumerian Goddess.

> In the Greco-Roman world, the Mother of the Gods has an assortment of names and attributes evolved from

combination of early tribal religions. Viewed as the divine intercessor between humanity and a wrathful, judgmental male deity, the Shekinah is ultimately linked to Isis, Mary, Sophia, and Mary Magdalene, all known as the Queens of Heaven.[45]

The unified religion of the Mother Goddess has long since disappeared, but deep within every woman is an unquenchable longing to return to the transcendent vision of wholeness, potency, and love of the Divine Mother. Wounded women feel validated and justified by identifying with a goddess. Predictably, She has been retained in the collective unconscious or the DNA of humanity. Jennifer Woolger notes that even though the Goddess must often travel in disguise these days, she is nonetheless still the Queen of Heaven and a force to contend with. "Despite Her continued denigration or disguise, the Goddess is still very much around, exercising a powerful influence in our lives."[46] Another author, Shirley Nicholson, sees that influence not a negative one as that of Eve the Temptress, complicit in every "fall," but as an uplifting, nurturing, and inspiring one.

> All their exoteric religions have personified it as a Goddess, an archangel mother of universes, races, nations, and humans. These personifications of the World Mother are among the very noblest concepts of the human mind, which in creating, reverencing, and serving them reaches its highest degree of idealism, devotion, and religious expression.[47]

Today, the Goddess movement the world over is expanding, promoting love, peace, and equal justice, especially for the oppressed. It strongly encourages everyone to understand the sacredness and sadness of our common planetary home in order to respond to our planet's ecological crisis. By connecting to Divine Feminine wisdom, humanity can be emboldened to courageous action to remedy its problems. As Andrew Harvey puts it, "She is the invisible spirit guiding human consciousness; a hidden presence longing to be known, calling out to the world for recognition and response."[48] A wise response to that call could lead to a great spiritual renewal. Joy F. Reichard also hears it as a call to love and respect the planet. She writes:

> The resurgence of the Sacred Feminine is very much a grassroots movement that is moving gradually into the establishment. Her message is one of love for fellow beings, cooperation, compassion, care for the young, and respect for the care of the planet, which is Her body.[49]

The Goddess is reappearing in many unexpected places today with a dynamic, ongoing presence. She is a mother and a wife, and there is nothing docile about her. Indeed, She is an archetype of female concern and strength. When she encounters something out of balance, she fixes it, leaving nothing undone. Amazingly, She has kept the world together through Her strong will and compassion. British author J. Lyn Studebaker goes one step further and, with history as proof, implies that the early female leaders were perhaps our best because they led us to live together in peace and harmony. She writes: "But of all the praises that can be sung about our Great-Goddess ancestors, probably the most stunning of all is their ability to live for hundreds, maybe thousands of years without plunging into the hell that is human warfare."[50] Joy F. Reichard sees the re-emergence of the ways of the Goddess as a return to a saner, healthier, earth-based spirituality, and a pathway to that long-lost peace. She illuminates:

The goddess is becoming: a metaphor for the earth as a living organism, an archetype for feminine consciousness, a mentor for healers, the emblem for a new political movement, an inspiration for artists, a model for re-sacralizing the female body and the mystery of human sexuality and a catalyst for an emerging spirituality that is earth-centered.[51]

Goddess thought challenges biblical and so-called "traditional" ideas about the nature of God. The Goddess inference also challenges religious historians to abandon their almost exclusive commitment to text, requiring them to accept physical evidence such as paintings, sculptures, bones, pots, weavings, etc. as reliable evidence upon which to build theory. Little by little, people are remembering the Goddess. It is as if scripture and writing in general have become a wall, blocking off access to pre-literate understandings of the universe, understandings that included a female deity at its core. Many are still dissecting that wall, longing to break through. As Carol Christ observes, "As we learn about ancient Goddess religions and cultures, we begin to understand that we do not have to live in a culture that worships one male God, where the domination and control of women, earth, and other people are taken for granted and warfare is perpetual."[52] Tricia McCannon emphasizes the non-singularity of the feminine deity, honoring a great plurality of names and forms, all good, and all aspects of one creative force that lies behind all life's illusions. She points out:

Throughout the centuries, the Goddess has been known by many different names in many different cultures. In Christianity she is called Mary, the great mother of compassion. In Judaism she is known as Sophia, the

Goddess of Wisdom. In India, she is Lakshmi, the Mother of Generosity who dwells in the Great Cosmic Egg with Vishnu, Her eternal mate. She is also Sarasvati, the Goddess of Creativity, and Durga, the vanquisher of demons. She is named Parvati, the Mother of the Universe, and Kali, the great transformer who rules the cycles of death and rebirth. In China, she is embodied in Quan Yin, the bodhisattva of children, and in Japan she is Amaterasu, the Goddess of the Sun. These are only a few of Her many faces.[53]

Today there is a progressive reshaping of myths, legends, traditions, and creation stories. A great cultural shift is proceeding that is slowly transitioning us back to a more gender-balanced culture. Yet it was only a relatively short time ago that popular opinion was reconsidered as a result of reassessing archeological sites and ancient texts. In fact, as goddess evidence expands, women's prestige, rights, and freedom are elevated and advanced. This proves, unmistakably, that the Goddess and women in general were co-opted, overlooked, and forgotten in the politics of patriarchy. Asphodel P. Long suggests, "Within what appears to be a totally patriarchal religious history, the female deity of Wisdom has remained hidden."[54] What she means is that the goddess is right there in front of us, hidden from view in this "man's world," and yet fully present, a treasure for us to discover, if we look beyond appearances. J. Lyn Studebaker tells us how to unmask these hidden goddesses. She offers this insight:

> The old goddesses have never abandoned us. They bubble up regularly from their subterranean hideaways but in disguise. King Arthur and Robin Hood for example are men of the Goddess. Cinderella, Sleeping Beauty, and many of our old fairy tales are tales of the Goddess. By unmasking the Goddess in these tales and rubbing the war-god tarnish off Her, we

can get important clues about the nature of our healthy old Goddess way of life.[55]

Humanity is discovering a new spiritual power within by reconnecting to the feminine sacred source of creation. This rekindling is slowly restoring our families and communities. Recent years have seen exponential growth in the outpouring of the feminine divine. The outcome has been producing a higher vibration that is raising humanity's consciousness which in turn leads to greater scientific breakthroughs and developments. Nancy Oakes refers to it as a growth of spiritual consciousness. She writes, "History will record this new period of time as the 'Great Awakening,' as millions of people followed the brilliant golden light, Sophia, into the new era."[56] The Rev. Dr. Karen Tate describes this new mindfulness as she asserts:

> The Goddess represents the limitless potential of our individual and collective minds. Goddess consciousness is about recognizing that life is precious and sacred and that by increasing the dignity and freedom of all living things, we increase our own. The Goddess is the symbol of the highest responsibility to one another.[57]

In the Goddess tradition, a personal Divine Mother is fully within the world and within us. She is both immanent and transcendent. Mother God is deeply related to everything in the world. This means she is affected in the depth of Her being by everything that exists and everything that happens in the world. She resonates with both our joy and our suffering. Author H. I. Austen urges us to embrace this joy and suffering in order to live fuller lives. She writes, "Goddesses represent vital energies which we must reclaim if we are to live full and harmonious lives."[58]

In essence, the Divine Feminine is embedded in the sacredness and beauty of everything around us, while the Divine Masculine impacts undeniably the higher planes of existence, both realms worthy of our exploration.

> The sacred wholeness of life belongs to the feminine aspect of the divine, the Great Goddess. For Her, every act is sacred; every blade of grass, every creature is a part of the Great Oneness. In contrast to His awe-inspiring transcendence, She embodies the caring divine presence.[59]

Men and women are finally starting to realize that there is more to spirituality than what they have been taught. One reason is that Mother God is everything that is fathomed and still unfathomed. The liberation of Mother God as the Divine Feminine Goddess is causing a revolution that is gently transforming the planet back to the original ideal. Her invisible energy is circulating throughout the universe as the ultimate unifier of creation. "The Goddess is always attempting to persuade us to love intelligently, concretely, and inclusively."[60] Considering that women are now learning their rightful power and position, men will have to learn to be humble before feminine love and compassion. Clearly, we all need to learn to accept Her help if we are to prosper as a civilization.

Chapter 2
Where Did She Go?

What really happened to the Divine Feminine? She cannot just have disappeared for no reason. One way or another, She was driven underground and lost to history. The largest contributing factor was probably the patriarchal religious systems that sanctioned ethics that elevated man over woman as well as God the Father over God the Mother. The maternal deity was neglected and then abolished, putting an end to humanity's divine gender harmony. As a result, Mother God was disregarded and scorned. Since then, there has been no lack of effort to eradicate all vestiges of goddess worship. In fact, in the last few thousand years there has been an almost complete authoritarian patriarchal system. McCannon describes a stark contrast between our ancient and recent histories in this regard when she writes, "The Mother Goddess, once venerated as the Giver of Life and the Welcomer of the Dead, was thrown down."[61] Ken Wilbur suggests that it isn't hard to find evidence of this tendency in Western literature; it's right there on the surface.

> The historical fact – not even hidden in mythology – is that the feminine principle was totally excluded from the newly emergent world of rational mind, of culture, of free communicative exchange. The primary injunction of the female was to be seen not heard.[62]

By contrast, in the early Neolithic era, many societies had woman-centered social structures, well-organized cities, highly sophisticated and beautiful art with no evidence of warfare. Women were respected and even accorded reverence, as the primary deity of that time was a multifaceted Goddess. Many early civilizations were based on a partnership between men and women and were brought to an end with the invasion by patriarchal tribes riding horses and armed with bronze weapons. These aggressive tribes then imposed their gods, their economy, and their hierarchical social structure on these fairly peaceful societies. People were not only told that the new male god would punish them for worshiping a female deity but that such activity was evil and immoral. This brainwashing campaign didn't stop a thousand or even a hundred years ago, but according to author William Bond, continues today. He writes, "There is still good reason to believe that the elimination of knowledge about matricentric societies still goes on."[63] Tricia McCannon believes this power shift to the men-only club has brought aggression into every aspect of our lives. She tells it like it is:

> For nearly two thousand years, the Western World has been taught almost exclusively about God the Father, and this masculine biased theology has shaped our use of language, law, culture, and property rights, teaching the values of aggression, dominance, and superiority of cultures around the world.[64]

The contrast between angry sky god cultures and gentler earth goddess peoples, which McCannon mentions, was most visible when European explorers began to "instruct" and conquer Native North Americans in the 1500s and 1600s. We are still recovering from that theological clash. It was natural for the earliest people worldwide to relate to Nature as Mother Earth, since the earth provided everything needed to subsist. It was also natural for people to worship the Mother Goddess and to see women in Her likeness. How and when did humanity lose this system of belief? Stories, scriptures, and folklore were rewritten so that the Goddess and women were pulled down. To have divine parental confidence weakened and obliterated has been both painful and traumatic for humanity. Author Carol Christ can still feel the pain of those who were first put to the sword of patriarchal dogma. She comments: "On the symbolic level, the Genesis story tells us that the Mother of All the Living, the Sacred Snake, and the Sacred Tree are the source of suffering. The authors of the Genesis story, like the authors of myths and epics, wrote with the deliberate intention of discrediting the worship of the Goddess."[65]

> Over time, history has concealed the feminine and mothering qualities of God. Who our Creator really is has been camouflaged innumerable times either partially, completely, sometimes intentionally, and sometimes unintentionally. The promotion of a totally male God has devalued motherhood, not only in society but also in their self-worth.[66]

The polytheistic worship of a Divine Mother and Father was sustainable for thousands of years giving positive role models to both genders. In time, however, the guardian Mother became less acceptable and ultimately ceased to exist in the minds of the high-ranking and influential. Women lost more and more power as men projected a negative image of women as deceptive, lying, and sexual. In the end, the patriarchal side suppressed the appearance and expression of the feminine. Joy Reichard does see hope but with a temporary transition into forgetfulness. She writes, "The Goddess isn't dead. It's just that many of us have forgotten about her; forgotten why the Divine Feminine was and is important."[67]

> The Christian Church may have taken the feminine out of the godhead, but it could not eradicate the Goddess

from people's hearts. The Goddess is alive and well now for the greatest number of Christians across the planet, as she was before Christianity even appeared. All that has changed is her name. Many of her functions and characteristics have remained unchanged.[68]

In contrast to the continued onslaught of patriarchal authority, author Barbara G. Walker chooses the female deity over the male, citing the mother as the highly visible source of life, nurturing, and trust in each person's life.

> "The only religious symbol that makes rational sense is the Goddess-as-Mother, since the natural teacher and authority figure for every young mammal - including the human one - is none other than the mother. The relationship of child to mother is the foundation of all love, trust, dependence, and yearning for guidance."[69]

There are few reliable records of how exactly the ancient matriarchal religions were supplanted. Since the feminine aspect of God has hardly been mentioned from biblical times to the present, it is safe to say that religions of today may have contributed to the denial or demonization of the Goddess. The great American feminist Elizabeth Cady Stanton wrote in 1896: "The Bible and Church have been the greatest stumbling blocks in the way of women's emancipation....the whole tone of Church teaching in regard to women is contemptuous and degrading....the religious superstitions of women perpetuate their bondage more than all other adverse influences."[70] One scholar who fought open battle against the masculinization of Christianity, and who for many readers literally rewrote history, was Elaine Pagels, author of *The Gnostic Gospels*. In this shocking but well-researched sourcebook of suppressed knowledge, she discloses:

Every one of the secret texts, which the Gnostics revered, was omitted from the canonical collection, and branded as heretical by those who called themselves orthodox Christians. By the time the process of sorting the various writings ended – probably as late as the year 200 – virtually all the feminine imagery for God had disappeared from orthodox Christian tradition.[71]

It is hardly surprising that many of the Hebrew prophets held it to be their religious task to turn their people from the worship of the Canaanite goddesses, both on the grounds of political expediency and following Yahweh's instruction to worship no idols. The way goddess images were actually worshiped was contrary to the whole feeling of the Old Testament religion, which was engaged in withdrawing participation from the images themselves in order to inspire consciousness beyond anything that can be represented in nature. Anne Baring writes, "Yahweh's holy war against the goddess eventually became implicitly a paradigm of opposition, of good against evil, of masculine against feminine."[72] Ironically, Abraham's, the son of an idol maker, decided to follow a single monotheistic God which developed into the destruction and demonization of all other choices. Merlin Stone urges us to do our own research and to follow the trail of others' search for the facts in this matter.

It is time to bring the facts about the early female religions to light. They have been hidden away too long. With these facts we will be able to understand the early development of Judaism, Christianity, and Islam and their reactions to the female religions and customs that preceded them. With these facts we will be able to understand how these reactions led to the political attitudes and historical events that occurred as these male-oriented religions were forming – attitudes and events that played such a major part in formulating the image of women during and since that time.[73]

What Stone implies is that we cannot trust common knowledge or even our own guesswork because we ourselves have been so misinformed. The process of weeding out truth from lies is slow and laborious, but the need for actualities is immediate. The one-sidedness of a primarily masculine deity has brought humankind to the point of moral disintegration. Without feminine influence, efficient functionality in society has fallen apart, bringing about injurious and even devastating impacts. Unless we bring back the feminine powers of intuition, the organic integration of the universe will turn out to be a thing of the past. As a result of banning the healing powers of the sacred feminine, our culture has taken away our intrinsic self, our true heart, and our true wealth. Reverend Dr. Tate states poetically, "When the Queen steps forward with Her vision, Her ability to receive, Her boundaries, and Her leadership, all the ills of the world begin to fall away."[74] She is not referring to the Queen of England but to all forms of the Queen of Heaven, of which there are many. In spite of this rich variety of goddesses to be honored, author Barbara G. Walker laments the fact that almost every American has been indoctrinated in single-minded patriarchal dogma to some degree, and brought up in ignorance of the Divine Feminine in all Her forms. She observes:

> Nearly every American woman now alive was taught in her childhood that God is male. She was given no opportunity to grow up with a generally accepted idea of feminine divinity. It was only in adulthood that some women have come to recognize the Goddess as a primary and primordial metaphor of the sacred, both

within themselves and in the shadowed areas of history and prehistory.[75]

Fear about whatever threatened their authority was used by the early Church to keep people in the dark. The early Church did not want anyone to acknowledge Mother God because that would have given Her power. Gnostic Christianity honored both the male and female aspects of the Creator, yet the early Church kept this knowledge a secret. The role of Mary Magdalene as Jesus' chief apostle, as described in Elaine Pagel's *Gnostic Gospels,* and other works, was entirely deleted, as were most references to the Divine Feminine. The early Christians continued to honor the feminine aspect of God until the Council of Nicea replaced Her with only the masculine version of God. After that, secret societies that venerated the feminine had to go underground to survive. Uncovering explanations on why the Goddess and the female tradition were obscured can only be done by reevaluating history. This conspiracy could have been accomplished only with the use of fear, and sometimes by force. Sylvia Brown writes, "Gnostics needed to hide their knowledge of Mother and Father God due to persecution by the patriarchal power structure."[76] Anne Baring stresses that the Gnostic Goddess was not opposed to the existence of the male deity, but in fact was married to Him.

> Gnostic Christianity retained the tradition and image of Sophia as the embodiment of Wisdom. She was the Great Mother, the consort and counterpart of the male aspect of the godhead. When the Gnostic sects were repressed by the edicts of the Emperor Constantine in AD 326 and 333, the image of Sophia as the embodiment of Wisdom was again lost.[77]

By the beginning of the Christian era, the Goddess, often called Sophia, was beginning to be portrayed as the feminine dimension of the divine and even as the savior for the Jewish people. There was no question that this female aspect of God rivaled the power of Yahweh as Her words stopped men in their tracks, since they had all the marks of the divine. Her role in the divine mystery was embellished when She commanded men to choose between life and death. Still, Her image and messages are sometimes fraught with confusion, as it was not clear if she was a Goddess or a representative of the Divine Feminine. Carol Schaefer explains this confusion as perhaps a product of Her widespread cross-cultural appearances when she writes: "Her manifestations are not confined to any specific people, place, belief, or time."[78] Author Alix Pirani foresees this confusion returning with the reawakening of the feminine power, and is perfectly comfortable with that. She reflects:

> The rediscovery of the Goddess not only involves the development of new ideas, new symbols, new rituals, maybe new religions, but a reappraisal of the past. Thus, throughout the history of the Christian Church, there have been rich veins of feminine spirituality and mysticism, often ignored or demeaned, that we are able to reevaluate today as manifestations of the slumbering Goddess.[79]

Sophia was pushed out of the early Church's life by various writers who did not give much attention to Her real identity in biblical texts. The orthodox male view of women tended to dominate these writings, since most of the texts were composed by men who were denied access to information about women. The thoughts and experiences of women were usually omitted or slanted, as male control of religion was common. To compensate for some of these omissions, She was illustrated in several medieval manuscripts. However, Mother God's strong influence empowered women too much for the male priesthood, thus threatening the existing church hierarchy. Barbara G. Walker implies that the priests would do anything to disempower women in the church, including making up false accounts of divine guidance. "As long as modern society continues to give its official recognition to an exclusive male deity and its moral standards are set by men who pretend to have been instructed by that deity, it will continue to be a patriarchy."[80] Carol Schaefer believes that such priests and ministers are only hurting themselves and that wounding their own feminine side will only further separate them from spirit. Sympathetically, she observes:

> It is time for the male religious leaders to stop overlooking half the human race and include women voices to their dialogue and decisions. They would serve themselves well if they would learn to develop the feminine side of themselves that is already part of their own nature.[81]

Even though Mother God has long been forgotten, She has not forgotten Her children. She was rejected since She does not condone dishonorable human behavior. She was too big to fit neatly into organized discussions of divinity, even though She is on equal status with God the Father. Nonetheless, throughout religious and even non-religious history, Mother God in all Her representations was still depicted as the divine, life-saving female figure. She has countered evil through influencing society with an unseen feminine wholesomeness. "Goddess spirituality is not restrained by orthodoxies of custom or culture but can realistically address issues of economy, justice, ecology, education, racial, sexual, and species inequality."[82]

Many renowned people in the past have thought of God in both masculine and feminine terms. Hildegard of Bingen of the twelfth century believed God's maternal love opened us to repentance. Carl Jung felt that true equality between men and women would be tied to acceptance of a concrete, personal divine woman. Albert Einstein once said that Israel would not experience salvation until it returned to feminine divinity. Nikola Tesla said the struggle toward equality of the sexes will end with the female as superior with the awakening of the intellect of women. Carol Schaefer correctly stated, "Women carry the ancient knowledge of the Divine Feminine deep within the very cells of their being."[83]

This feminine form of intelligence has long been said to differ from that of the male. Mythology tends to show Goddesses approaching problems more imaginatively than the Gods. Although too complex to discuss here, recent research has revealed the "female brain" works very differently than the "male brain." It has been described as more abstract and less compartmentalized. Anne Baring describes this difference theologically:

> For the last 4,000 years, the feminine principle, which manifested in mythological history as the 'goddess' with values placed upon spontaneity, feeling, instinct, and intuition, had been lost as a valid expression of the sanctity and unity of life. In Judeo-Christianity, there is formally no feminine dimension of the divine, since our culture is structured in the image of a masculine God who is beyond creation, ordering it from without; He is not within creation, as were the Mother Goddesses before Him. The result, inevitably, is an imbalance of the masculine and feminine principles, which has

fundamental implications for how we create our world and live in it.[84]

Sooner or later, the time will come when men and women will stand together as equals. The only viable hope for this to happen is when feminine values under Mother God reestablish a higher moral ground for humanity to stand on. Today, there are more settings than ever before where Mother God can express, share, and network Her viewpoint. Before the Internet, there was little chance for women and men worldwide to share, confide, and promote their faith in the feminine aspect of God's nature. Alix Pirani suggests that humanity's inability to conceptualize the universe as both male and female has complicated the theological discussion and similarly damaged human relationships. She declares, "So the lost feminine element and the usurping hyper-masculine element have been a key problem for both men and women and have bedeviled relations between them."[85]

Is it possible for the female spirit to lead humanity, given that men have been leading politically, economically, and spiritually for such a long time? The present system and structure have produced many social evils, including war, poverty, exploitation, servitude, greed, fear, and corruption. Since humanity has not figured out how to get it all quite right, perhaps it is time to look down another road? Today, some women feel that a return to the ancient concept of Goddess supremacy is essential to the process of healing the wounds of the modern world. Many people are starting to realize they should not question women's sincerity and spiritual authority. In *She Who Is,* author Elizabeth A. Johnson throws down the gauntlet in defense of all that is feminine, stating: "Whenever women are violated, diminished, have their life drained away,

God's glory is dimmed and put at historical risk."[86] Her warnings should be reflected upon and taken seriously in this twenty-first century.

> The human race began with the Divine Mother and, despite a long tragic journey away from Her, must return to Her. The Divine Mother wants the human race to embody complete freedom, with the living knowledge of innate divinity. The next stage of human development can unfold through impassioned cocreation and participation in the will, love, and power of the sacred feminine.[87]

People naturally interpret the feminine nature of God against the background of the God they know. It is difficult to understand Mother God without comparing Her to the images of God in our inherited religious traditions. Up until now, the concept of a masculine God was the most prevalent understanding, according to biblical images and their Christian and Jewish interpretations. For these and other problematic reasons, most people have never been told about Mother God. Since She doesn't really exist in Western culture, people who believe in and talk about Mother God are considered mistaken and annoying. Carol Christ reflects the experience about this when she states, "Most people become flustered, upset, and even angry when it is suggested that the God they know as Lord and Father might also be called 'God the Mother' or 'Goddess.'[88]

Chapter 3
What Will Happen When She Reappears?

Janet Wolter and Alan Butler remark prophetically in *America, Nation of the Goddess*:

> A mere millennium and a half ago, after maybe a hundred thousand years of adoration, an effort was made to extinguish the Great Goddess from the Abrahamic faiths, but it was an attempt doomed to failure.[89]

Whatever the reason, it is clear that Mother God's influence was gradually diminished and replaced by a masculine figure. After this shift, direct access to the Divine Feminine was cut off and repressed, so She was forced underground where She stayed in the collective unconscious. After that, the groundwork for Her return came in archetypes of disguised or hidden forms. Author Karen Speestra hands us the blueprint for locating Her in this day and age, and it is in the disguise she has worn for centuries that we find her. She says, "We look for other places to 'read' her. She's in nature, sacred geometry, folk dances, symbols, fairy tales, and within our own bodies."[90] Nancy Oakes suggests that it is imperative that we find Her, now that the hour of Her return has come.

> Spiritually she has always been with Her creation, within the eternal soul of humanity. She has assigned many angels, guides, and reincarnated souls to lead humanity over the many past centuries. However, Her return speaks to Her understanding of the perilous danger that is capable of destroying Her creation and the planet. With all Her power from the highest heavens and those that align and unite with her, she arrives to defend Her creation.[91]

Although awareness of the Divine Mother went astray, there were camouflaged signs of Her presence, leading to Her reintegration back into society. Her spirit is still swelling like yeast within the reformed streams of established religions. Mystics of all faiths are starting to recognize the Divine Feminine as the lost connection between this world and the next. Yet, mainstream culture and media have not fully endorsed a resurgence of interest in the Divine Feminine. Caitlin Matthews describes this lost connection as a wound we must heal. "The loss of the Divine Feminine from consciousness is a wound that we all carry."[92] Author Karen Speestra reminds us that all true goddesses have feelings, and that Sophia, among others, must be feeling somewhat downcast as a result of all that has happened in the last few thousand years. She reflects:

> Sophia has reason to be more than a little miffed. For the last several centuries, Sophia has been repressed, banished, outlawed, and forbidden. Her name has been scrubbed off scriptural parchments and deleted from computer screens. Her sacred groves have been cut down and burned. Her priestesses eliminated. In the wake of Her departure, 'Father-figure-gods' began to dominate all the major religions around the world.[93]

Once Her presence is re-established, the feminine principle will begin to spread out rapidly. At the hour women awaken to the Divine Feminine, they will permanently change their self-identity. One might ask, "If She is so powerful, and we are Her children, why can't She just take back the helm and redirect humanity?" For the sake of honoring our free will, and to respect our individual growth and learning process, this space-giving Mother God will not respond until She is called upon.

When Her children honor Her, She feels motivated and empowered. Some day, we will turn to Her for help, and at that time, the intercession of Mother God will bring about the dawning of a new age.

Popular author Sylvia Browne feels that in biblical times and in the early Western church, men who had just taken the helm were in fear of losing it to a "new age" in their own time. She writes, "Men in those early days feared the emotion and abilities of women, and they did not want any woman to know that there could be a feminine part of God because that would empower the female."[94] We still see the same thing today, with hidden messages in the media that direct our thoughts away from egalitarian, compassionate ways of looking at the world. In *She Lives,* a book by Rev. Jann Aldredge-Clanton, the author states that everyone needlessly struggles with the consequences of this oppression.

> Because the Feminine Divine is oppressed in the world, feminine energy - with traits of compassion, nurturing, creating, and community - is oppressed. Therefore, everyone, including white men, suffers to some degree. Creating ways to allow a greater number of people access or means to connect to the Feminine Divine and validate the Feminine Divine within each of us will consequently bring about a shift of consciousness to tolerance, social justice, and respect for the Earth and Her resources.[95]

Spiritual changes have caused a dramatic spiritual shift, causing major changes in the way people think about life. Eventually, it will become more obvious that Mother God is behind the events of the day. Perhaps the collapse of values, the breakdown of paradigms, and the destruction of traditions are happening so that humanity can wake up and really listen. Eventually, only faith in Mother God can heal and empower Her children with a renewed spirituality that will give birth to a new world. Robert Powell and Estelle Isaacson see Sophia as something of a savior-like figure for future humanity, and exclaim, "The coming down of Sophia from celestial heights is our hope, joy, and our source of comfort for the future."[96] Elsewhere in their book *The Mystery of Sophia,* they proclaim further:

> Mother God is inspiring many aspects of a new world culture, including: true interreligious unity, creating a brotherhood/sisterhood between all peoples, social justice, revealing the history of humanity's spiritual evolution, unity and harmony of the planet as a world community, economic well-being for every man, woman, and child on the planet, enabling education so that each person's creativity can unfold, and the spiritualization of the planet.[97]

In this new view, the only hell to fear is the one we have created for ourselves in Her absence. Something other than dogma and humdrum conventionality is beckoning humanity to seek Mother God as a mother and guide. Concerned, conscientious, and perceptive people are now studying feminine remedies never considered before. Once women around the world assemble and share with a common spiritual consciousness, there no longer will be a vacuum in which evil can strike. Through this process, Mother God will establish and sustain female dignity and rights through the full participation of women in society. Susan Cady wrote, "Sophia brings women strength and nurture for the struggle and upholds them in the midst of difficulty. She unlocks the power which has been accessible only through male symbols of the divine and shares it with those who have been shut out."[98] This is more true now than when Cady's book, *Wisdom's Feast,* was released in 1986. The word is spreading, and not just through the "grapevine" of feminism. It is starting to impact the whole world.

Even now, feminine divinity is ancestrally accepted as part of the ongoing tradition of belief in only a few parts of the world. Women in these cultures naturally feel stronger, more empowered, and more self-assured. When Mother God is reintroduced to our Western society, women will once again feel spiritually intuitive and confident as well. The outcome will benefit the world over. Sylvia Browne reveals a remarkable truth, surprising at least to many Americans, when she writes, "All indigenous people from the African continent have this tremendous love of Mother Earth, Mother God. Compared to our society, these so called primitive people have less mental illness and sickness, and hardly any insanity."[99] Anne Baring reveals a possible reason why this belief in the Divine Feminine is so healthy for us when she declares:

> The Mother Goddess, wherever she is found, is an image that inspires and focuses a perception of the universe as an organic, alive, and sacred whole, in which humanity, the Earth and all life on Earth participate as 'Her children.' Everything is woven together in one cosmic web where all orders of manifest and unmanifest life are related, because all share in the sanctity of the original source.[100]

When civilization behaves barbarously, society declines and despairs. Only when women come together for a common, higher ideal can they redirect society purposefully. The natural spiritual authority to lead humanity toward goodness will develop once women recognize the value of Mother God as a role model. Nothing less than a total reversal of the exploitative attitude toward nature and women has any chance of resetting the balance so that the world can reach a happy equilibrium. Vajra Ma stresses that such healing is not just for the individual, but also for groups of people, and indeed the world. She says, "For when women come together in a group with a spiritual intent, there is that collective consciousness, a deep mind that arises from a hidden stream, a fountain of deep wisdom that is bigger than just one individual mind and its concepts, of a scope beyond present time and contemporary experience."[101] Vajra Ma's words echo in harmony with those of Carol Schaefer, who sees this happening soon and on a global scale. She pleads:

> With the world on the brink of destruction, women must wake up this great force they possess and bring the world back to peace and harmony. When women and men set in motion this enormously transformative feminine force of unconditional love they carry within, great healing and change will come about.[102]

Changing our language and pictures to incorporate the feminine nature of God is critical for changing our current attitudes and patterns. After Mother God is accepted, the sacred balance of the male and female can be restored. Stress and anxiety will fade naturally as humanity regains trust once again. With this new vibration of love forgiveness, humanity will shed the discriminations and imbalances of the past. Nancy Oakes writes, "This return of the 'Sacred Mother' energy is the deliverance and healing for a very sick planet and people."[103] Robert Powell also shares this emerging belief in planetary salvation through Her, when he recommends:

Sophia is someone who enables us to begin to discover who we are, what we think, what we feel, and what we are able to do, on a much deeper level than we can possibly imagine. We have forgotten the ability to appreciate the multidimensional aspects of existence. Through our scientific technological civilization, we have lost this heartfelt relationship to existence and we need to find it again. Sophia is the one who can help us do this.[104]

Relatively few people have come to this simple but deep understanding of God's profound parental nature. The image of the universe as the body of Mother God challenges the traditional view of God. This means that God is part of every being and everything that happens in the world. As fully embodied in and related to the world, God feels all the joy and pain that Her children go through. As a living presence in the world, God suffers with our suffering and rejoices in our joy. Carol Christ says, "A theology that envisions the Earth as the body of the Goddess will recognize, appreciate, and celebrate the great diversity of life within the Earth body."[105] This inclusive view is shared and expanded upon in Andrew Harvey's vision of the Divine Feminine. He exclaims:

The Divine Mother is showing the world Her most marvelous miracle of all: that normal life is compatible with supreme realization, and that direct mystical contact with the divine, with Her, can be sustained in any setting or activity. This is the revolution that She is offering, a revolution that could dissolve all dogmas and hierarchies without exception; all separation whatever between ordinary and spiritual life, the sacred and the profane, the mundane and the mystical.[106]

We are entering a new era where Mother God is attempting to become more and more a part of our lives.

Mother God, in Her many roles and representations, is covertly and overtly returning everywhere, including in academia, business, philosophy, religion, science, and politics. Also, She is there as a source of help and inner strength for each person's problems and questions. "The Goddess speaks our language and has answers that are suitable to our times."[107] God as Mother cares for the well-being of the entire Earth, which is Her household. Because Mother God desires to see the spiritual fulfillment of the whole, interconnected world, Her attention is turned in a special way toward the ones who are most in need. She loves the weak and dispossessed as much as She loves the strong and beautiful.

Reclaiming God's feminine nature can be identified as a "eureka" moment for both women and men. Experiencing the freely moving, life-giving, feminine spirit of Mother God connects, renews, and blesses everyone in contact with Her. When this happens, there will be a feminist revival and a regaining of the divine presence. Another benefit is that Father God's spirit is uplifted and completed with the introduction and inclusion of God's femininity. "Recognizing feminine qualities within God enhances His image as Father to God the Heavenly Parent."[108] Powell and Isaacson foresee with great expectations the continual expansion of this truly divine influence in the affairs of humankind when they assert:

> We are entering an age when the female soul will become ever purer and broader, when ever-greater numbers of women will become profound inspirers, sensitive mothers, wise counselors, and far-sighted leaders. It will be an age when the feminine in humanity will manifest itself with unprecedented strength, striking a perfect balance with masculine impulses.[109]

There is no more gripping image of female power than Mother God. She understands the many intricacies of the web of life and embodies unconditional love. She represents a deep connection to the past, present, and future. Carol Christ speaks of a great healing and unification of all aspects of life when she writes, "The return of the Goddess inspires us to hope that we can heal the deep rifts between women and men, between man and nature, and between God and the world, that have shaped our Western view of reality for too long."[110] Nancy Oakes, in *Return of Sophia,* strikes a similar chord of hope in expressing:

> The "Great Mother" is the Source, the womb from which all creation springs. This truth is understood by all indigenous cultures. This clarification is the reappearance of the "Great Mother" into Her rightful spiritual and creative position within the creation story. Vanishing centuries of elimination, disconnection, belittlement, and oppression of the Source of human creation, She has returned.[111]

Mother God is enraged that it is taking so long for Her children to understand this fundamental truth, without which Her world is spiraling into irreversible darkness and destruction. Only by doing the spiritual work of transforming consciousness to a new divine reality of life can the original divine plan be advanced. A relationship needs to be re-established in which men take a humbler part and where women's voices and experiences are taken into account. Although Mother God is sweet, loving, and generous, She is frustrated that we are still internally asleep. We have not discovered Her phenomenal female nature that allows us to better appreciate and embrace life. Asphodel Long sees the Great Mother as the architect of the cosmos, willing to impart its secrets. She contends: "We have seen as architect and contriver of the universe , She knows its secrets and will share them with humanity."[112]

We have been denied an understanding of Feminine Spirit and have been nurtured on only divine masculine values. We each need to break our old spiritual paradigms in order to discover our true relationship with Mother God. When we connect to Mother God, we connect to the wisdom of the cosmos. When we have gender balance among ourselves and in our relationship with heaven, we can better follow our divine heart. McCannon focuses on how the feminine principle weaves everything together when she writes: "The mother exists within the matrix, and all things are woven within her. She is not absent from the world but alive within everything, in both seen and unseen dimensions. Such an image helps us to honor the sacred in everything, fostering compassion and kindness to all."[113] Reverend Dr. Karen Tate emphasizes the importance of what type of language we use to refer to the Divine Feminine. She instructs:

> Exclusively masculine divine language and symbolism devalue the feminine by ignoring it. Divine Feminine symbolism and language are vital to the revaluing of females. Since male and female are in the divine image, as Genesis 1:27 states, the divinity includes the female and should be named and imaged as female.[114]

Tate is referring to a passage in chapter five of the first book of the Bible that states, "When God created man, He made him in the likeness of God. *Male and female created He them.*" Pretty strong stuff. And yet this reference is largely ignored or misinterpreted. When we use certain words, they imply a patriarchal lifestyle. Carol Christ calls on us to change the way we think; the way we access knowledge. She suggests, "Until and unless the sources of religious experience and knowledge are transformed, traditional understandings will be with us."[115]

> What would it be like if women emulated the femininity of God? What aspects of themselves would they discover worthy of praise? Would they be able to uplift one another? Liberated of the need to compete with other women for male approval, divinely inspired women could claim their own creative power. They would discover newer and larger arenas in which their feminine creativity could flourish. Following Sophia's lead, women would be free to voice their anger and impatience with society's injustice.[116]

The image and vision of the Divine Feminine has appeared in all of the religious traditions, yet Mother God is far beyond all concepts, doctrines, and creeds. She is above religion, race, nationality, and gender. Regardless of time or place, She is patient yet rigorous, gentle yet stern, just yet forgiving. Maybe the easiest way to come to understand and connect with Mother God is watching how a baby or child relates to its mother.

Chapter 4
How Do I Relate with Mother God?

Could this be the answer to humanity's prayers? Is this a concept whose time has come? Will this revelation provide the vision that will give the whole world hope? The desire to be reunited with one's mother is an instinctual behavior pattern that is deeply imprinted on the human psyche. When one has a personal and intimate relationship with Mother God, one's soul is filled with new vitality. Amazingly, recognizing the feminine essence of God can be an overpowering surprise. Coming to have a personal and intimate relationship with Mother God permeates the soul with new vitality and is literally an "Oh My God!" moment. "Mother God has been patiently preparing for Her re-emergence onto the world stage, and into our daily lives as well."[117]

A new birth happens when Mother God's presence is felt. Since nothing like this has been explained in established religions, the experience can be especially overwhelming. When women and men become aware of Mother God their perception of reality changes. Previous concepts are altered into something that starts to make sense. Susan Cady captures this feeling when she writes, "The woman who finds God within herself and loves Her fiercely can now call Her by name, and the struggle will never be the same again."[118] The return of the Holy Spirit has long been awaited in Christian dialogue, but few realize it is really the feminine essence of God. A number of Christians are reawakening to the power of the Mother God linking them to ancient as well as native creation goddesses. "They may have different names, approaches, methods, and means to express this Divine Feminine nature, but the effect is the same."[119]

61

Most people cannot imagine that at this time in history the ultimate experience of becoming one with God is at hand. From the beginning, God has been continuously trying to dwell with humanity. Likewise, humanity has been trying to connect with God in an almost endless quest to locate their divinity. This new spirituality could result in prodigious external changes for humanity. Asphodel Long implies it is not just that humanity is suddenly so much wiser; it is that Mother is reaching out to us. Long writes, "Wisdom is making herself available to us all. We have no difficulty in seeking or finding her. Indeed, She herself seeks us."[120] Tim Bulkeley, in fact, suggests that we are still in a state of confusion concerning this feminine wisdom and how to speak of it. He spells it out candidly:

> Few of us are familiar or comfortable with talk of God as our 'heavenly mother'. We are so unfamiliar with the motherly language of God that when we come across it in the Bible, or the writings of early theologians, we often explain it away or deny it.[121]

While there have been limited conversations about Her intent and hopes, Mother God has been boxed out of the daily flow of communication. She has worked as a nameless face to recapture love for Her family and Herself. When the ability to understand God's female side is broadened, Her femininity will be expressed in ways never before understood. Needless to say, it has been impossible to create heaven on earth without Mother God. Asphodel Long attributes to Her considerable power to heal the planet. Long writes, "She is the all-pervading force of nature of which She is the source and which she orders and rules."[122]

Losing our connection to the Great Mother has weakened and skewed our attitude toward life. As a general rule, society has been one-sided, overemphasizing the masculine and not dealing fairly with the feminine. Some of the outcomes on a larger level have been violence, corruption, racism, poverty, and pollution. To help prove a relationship between the denial of Mother and our current problems, Jennifer Woolger examines those times when She was not denied her position in the spiritual sphere. She describes it simply, "Historians of religion agree that at those times in human history when the Great Mother was worshipped, human beings were very much in harmony with themselves and with the life force."[123] Popular author Sondra Ray explains how this gradual denigration of the Divine Feminine led step by step to our current state of affairs. She asserts:

> Since the Goddess has not been an integral part of Western life the last two thousand years, we as Her children are rather maladjusted. The Goddess, or Divine Mother, would lead us in the way of natural law, wisdom, and unconditional love; however, we don't pay enough attention to this aspect of God. That may be because of old beliefs that the Goddess is pagan and heathen. This is most unfortunate, because we then overlook Her beneficial, life-enhancing, and regenerative powers and Her offer of renewal.[124]

Despite the fact that Mother God has been denied, ignored, and excluded, She always finds a way of surviving the most restrictive of ideologies. She has been inching Her way into the recognized consciousness, especially in the last half century. Soon this period of Sacred Feminine repression will end. Then women can reclaim their lost power and rediscover their divine inheritance. Susan Cady describes this as a truly innovative, creative power when she writes, "Women can claim their own creative power in all its wonder and mystery - the power is theirs to bring into being new ideas, new projects, new ways of working and being together."[125]

Mother God teaches women how they can be empowered by fully identifying with Her. Though we yearn for the love of our Divine Parent we may feel inferior or not worthy. Yet, the highest level of piety is demonstrated when associating with God as a parent. Such a trust fosters humanity's innate desire for a complete maternal embrace, including the gratitude and reverence that accompany it. Humanity has a natural instinct to be children of the Most High. In *Gospel of the Goddess,* William Bond and Pamela Suffield imply that past doctrines concerning eternal sin, hell, and damnation have convinced us of our separation, but this is an illusion we can overcome. They expound, "None of us has ever left the Great Mother, though we may think we have. She is still protecting us, and preventing us from becoming stuck forever in our mistakes."[126] She embraces a unique relationship with each of Her children. When She makes Herself known, a profound emotional healing takes place.

At this time, Mother God is the divine catalyst to bridge heaven and earth. She is not only the Creator and source of life, She is our inner guide and intuitive helper. When we hear Her voice within, we find ourselves. It is as if a light bulb goes on in a dark room and everything becomes clear. This inexplicable experience mingles the physical with the spiritual, the mortal with the immortal. The Divine Feminine is not fixed or finite, but constantly moving and ongoing around us. Those who have contact with the mystical power of Mother God encounter something uncanny and beyond human understanding. Alix Pirani confirms this when stating, "We experience Her in subjective ways, but Her being is objective and beyond us all."[127] Andrew Harvey turns to the great Sri Aurobindo Ghose (1872-1950), author of *The Life Divine* and one of the most admired adherents to the Divine Mother in modern times, to describe for us what it is like to be reunited with Her in ecstasy. Harvey writes:

> What Aurobindo saw and knew from his own experience was that if we could align ourselves totally and passionately in love and dedication to the Divine Mother, it could transform all aspects of human life. It could transform not only our minds, illuminated by the ecstasy of the divine gnosis of the Mother; not only our hearts, opened to the unconditional boundless, tender, ecstatic love of the Mother; it would open our vision to the light coursing through all the various chakras and blazing above our heads.[128]

This is not to say that maintaining such ecstasy will be easy once we find it. It is only by passing through difficulties can we be continually remade in the image of Her love. When we realize that the lack of the Divine Feminine has allowed so much agony and grief, we can begin to let Her back into our lives. After we experience this heart of reunion, the conjoined aspects of tears and sweetness, we can value how to live in the heart of the Divine Mother. Andrew Harvey acknowledges this fact when he illuminates, "There is no escape from the fire of suffering, but by embracing its necessity completely, we can become one with it. Then we will discover that the fire of suffering is also the fire of love."[129]

Many people are angry, depressed, and lost in their own despair. Anyone going through the dark night of the soul faces an immense internal struggle. Where can one find the courage and strength to overcome great difficulties? Connecting with the mind and heart of Mother God supplies the power to burn away the illusions. The future will be unimportant unless we restore the divine childhood by restoring a sincere relationship with our Mother God. We shouldn't erect huge churches and monuments to Her, nor should we establish strict dogmas and doctrines to show respect for Her. In fact, Andrew Harvey goes as far as to say, "The Mother is trying to release us from all religious and political systems."[130]

Just as there is no Father without the Mother, there can be no God without the Goddess. The human psyche still longs for the experience of its first acknowledged parent. It may be said that the return to the image of the original Great Mother could ease the modern sense of alienation, as well as restoring to women their innate sense of worth. The mother figure affects people in a far different way than the father. Through the image of Sophia, women can affirm their own female identity and can claim full participation in society as a legitimate birthright.

Once humanity overcomes the shock of realizing what it has been missing, there will be a great transformation to make up for lost time. Since we are part of Mother God, we should feel no barriers, no fear; only joy and happiness. Everyone can experience a profound change through the love felt when the mind and spirit become free. This will be the final revolution to end hatred, inequality, and injustice. William Bond and Pamela Suffield write, "Having felt love from the Great Mother, they can never be quite the same again."[131] They suggest this change is intuitive and comes as a freeing of the spirit, an inner liberation that happens regardless of philosophical constructs or rules of conduct. They explain:

> Intuition is a gift from the Great Mother, a glimpse into unlimited possibilities from which we can choose according to our will. The gift comes without conditions and will not be withdrawn because of failure to meet some rules laid down by Her or Her representatives.[132]

Mother God elicits both pride and anger from women, a pride and anger they feel and very much need to express. Her presence helps women to value their own thoughts and feelings and to refuse to be silent or invisible. It is critically important to women that deity should have a female face, for humanity needs the comfort, strength, and spiritual support that only the Divine Feminine can give. The female side of God advocates for women affirming and protecting their bodies. Andrew Harvey describes the Divine Feminine in almost revolutionary terms when he writes, "What the Mother is doing all the time is trying to destroy the concepts of the mind, trying to destroy what destroys us: our separation, our dissociation, our vanity, our deluded sense of how we know the world, when in fact everything in this world is sacred and can only be known through love."[133] Paul R. Smith suggests that due to our conditioning from childhood, we need to develop a strong connection with the Divine Feminine before we can see through the illusions of patriarchal thinking and be free of them. He acknowledges his experience when he says:

> Perhaps one of the most profound changes in this journey comes when we abandon the old patriarchal divine images and come alive to God as woman – mother, sister, grandmother, friend, and lover. Until we

understand the feminine side of God, we don't know how to embrace the masculine side without getting entangled again in the old patriarchal images of divinity.[134]

Exclusively male images of God are killing the spirit by distorting the right understanding of masculinity and femininity. Images of God associated with authority and tenderness create a more accurate female image rather than a stereotype of how a woman ought to behave. The recognition of the biblical images of God as female, the infusion of positive female images into the language of faith, and the achievement of balance between male and female references will do a lot to bring renewed spiritual health. From just about any standpoint, it is essential to attribute both male and female characteristics to God. In spite of the inherent logic of this conclusion, God as the balanced parent has often been driven underground for centuries. As Long says, "The Mother-Father figure in divinity has come and gone throughout the ages."[135] Robert Powell and Estelle Isaacson and explain lucidly exactly how to conceptualize such a Divine Parent: not as a two-headed monster, but as two poles of a continuum of energy. One pole, the feminine, is grounded in our reality, and permeates our existence; the other, the masculine, is the transcendental source of all existence. They edify by imparting this thought:

In philosophical terms, we have, therefore, a transcendental aspect and an immanent aspect of the Godhead. In light of Sophia, the transcendental aspect would be called the Father. The immanent aspect of the Godhead would be called the Mother. We find, therefore, that the Mother can be conceived as the primordial substance of all creation. In the polarization within the Godhead at the beginning of creation, we find we can differentiate between the Creation, that is the Divine Mother, and that which is transcendental to the Creation, that is, the Divine Father.[136]

The soul's journey brings us continually and cyclically into the realm of the Father and then back to that of the Mother, and then to the Father again, in an endless dance of poise and balance along that band or continuum. The promise of bringing the divine masculine and feminine into balance within each human being will herald the dawning of a new age. It is Mother God's hope, as the mother of humanity, that Her children will enter into a new relationship with Her in an innovative and beneficial way. Her guiding influence will redress the imbalances caused by one-sided rational and scientific developments. She is now speaking directly in Her ageless wisdom as the comforter and caring mother of humanity. Caitlin Matthews refers to a virtual second coming of the divine within when she writes, "The seed of Sophia is within us all, waiting for the opportunity to manifest Her skillful wisdom in the world."[137] Reverend Dr. Karen Tate asserts an all-inclusive, balanced perspective when she explains the term Sacred Feminine does not imply that we should reject the Sacred Male, but embrace it as well. She writes:

> The Sacred Feminine is a concept that recognizes that "God" ultimately is neither anthropomorphically male or female but a Divine Essence beyond form and duality – an essence that is in balance and unification of masculine and feminine principles – a dynamic interdependent "Immanence" that pervades all life.[138]

The Motherly Heart of God may be compared with water that is soft yet capable of changing the surroundings, polishing stones to become nicely rounded with no sharp edges left, turning in this way a rough, jagged stone into a smooth one. Our Heavenly Mother works in our hearts, bringing about an all-encompassing healing. By learning and embracing the benevolent attitude of our Heavenly Parent, we can experience Her unconditional love toward others. We need the Divine Feminine to help us restore wholeness and to balance our understanding of God and our lives as well.

Chapter 5
Mother God: Parent and Role Model for Women

The revival of our concept and faith towards Mother God is unquestionably linked to recent breakthroughs for women, expanded ecological awareness, and increased interfaith activity. It is a slowly building movement that brings new freedoms and, like a breath of fresh air, a new way of examining life. Women, as well as men, are longing for God's feminine side to bring mercy and peace to the world. Viewing deity as female liberates everyone to discover a new love and to experience a deeper spirituality. Speaking of God as Mother solidifies the idea that family relationships are the principal way in which divine freedom is expressed. Cathy Pagano, author of *Wisdom's Daughters,* suggested that we can trust ourselves to Her when she wrote, "She is creator, wise in the ways of humanity, nature, and divinity."[139]

Even as gifted visionaries speak glowingly of Mother God, there is always the other side of the coin. If the prophets of the revival forget to mention both aspects of the Godhead, it is the limitations of language that cause them to overlook Him and Her. As Sylvia Browne points out:

> There have always been both a Mother and a Father God, so it is very hard to talk about one without the other. You are a pure energy force made by God; within you is imbued all aspects of Mother and Father God. Father God has both male and female aspects within Himself, and Mother God has both aspects. They are the archetypal figures of the feminine and masculine principles.[140]

God the Mother was part of various Gnostic communities, some of whom wrote about Her as the creative part of the male creator God. In the Gnostic Gospels, God is celebrated as God the Father/God the Mother. Members of at least one group of Gnostics received a secret tradition from Jesus to pray to both divine Father and Mother. The Gospel of the Holy Twelve reveals a prayer to the Divine Mother and Father. Tricia McCannon writes, "Today the only version of God that most people are familiar with is God the Father, yet Jesus referred to the Creator as the Abba/Amma or Father/Mother God. Among the many texts that speak about the Divine Father and Mother are the Gospel of Thomas, the Gospel of Philip, the Secret Book of John, the Gospel to the Hebrews, and the Sophia of Jesus Christ."[141] These are among the most widely read of the Gnostic gospels, and they firmly establish Gnosticism as a religion in which the Divine Feminine was central. Tricia McCannon quotes a lesser known Gnostic gospel called *The Humane Gospel*, but Jesus' message here is emphatic:

> In the Humane Gospel, we find Jesus speaking about the same Divine Mother and Father: Truly I say unto you, God is neither male nor female and yet both are one, and God is the Two in One. He is She and She is He. Therefore, I say unto ye, shall the name of the Father and Mother be equally hallowed and reverenced, for They are the great powers of God, and the one is not without the other in the One Infinite God.[142]

The Wisdom passages of Proverbs are often quoted to show that the Bible recognizes the existence of divine wisdom as the female aspect of God. Many of the great Mystery Schools of the past taught a balanced approach of yin and yang between men and women, creating role models for people to aspire to their own inherent divinity. Men and women both benefit when the feminine side of God is accepted as complementary to the masculine side. The banning of Gnostic texts in Western Europe in the late third century and the death penalty the Roman Empire placed on Gnostics in the fourth century did not stop the propagation of the Mother/Father God doctrine within Christianity. Tricia McCannon writes, "Beside the Gnostics, during the twelfth and thirteenth centuries, the Albigenses's, the Waldensians, the Cathars, and the Knights Templar honored the Divine Mother and Father."[143] These powerful groups were secretly preserving the Mother-Father deity, even through the Crusades, hidden sometimes within texts on alchemy and magic. Alan Butler in *City of the Goddess* says: "I hope the evidence I present will prove that Freemasonry is a hangover from the ancient mystery religions of Demeter and Isis...that all Freemasons are Goddess worshippers whether or not they realize it."[144]

The understanding of God as both male and female is radically different from what is ordinarily accepted. Yet, the significance of the unique image of God as fully feminine cannot be underestimated. The image of God as a mother who bonds with Her children while fulfilling many responsibilities is a source of great comfort and solidarity, especially for women. It has the ability to inspire and give hope to people worldwide, beyond the limitations of race, religion, or nationality. L. Juliana M. Claassens writes, "This image of God who weeps challenges our perceptions about the age-old question of theodicy."[145] Theodicy is a natural system of theology that seeks to vindicate divine justice in allowing evil to exist. How can God both eradicate all evil and encourage free will at the same time? It could be quipped that if God's main job is punishing evildoers, He is not doing a very good job. But if God's main job is to feel our pain, She has Her work cut out for Her. L. Juliana M. Claassens shares:

> This alternative metaphor of God as Wailing Woman challenges theological constructions of God in terms of divine retribution, which has dominated much of biblical interpretation. In the image of the Divine Mourner, God is perceived as being profoundly involved in suffering, sharing the pain experienced by the victims of trauma.[146]

Historically, wailing women were summoned in times when the traditional power structures of the community had fallen into disarray. In times of crisis, wailing women had the power to bring the community together in their grief. They could even rally a call against violence by raising their voices in protest against the injustice. Intuitively, women are strengthened by knowing that their pain and suffering are shared by a female God. L. Julia M. Claassens imparts, "Tears have a powerful way to break down barriers. Tears, particularly tears of compassion, can bring about healing where there used to be hatred or distrust."[147]

Jesus wept, but who would call him "weak?" The idea of extending God's comfort and love to others encourages us to think more broadly about the very nature of mothering. A mother's power is rooted in Her compassion. It flows from being deeply concerned with the needs of others. This female image of being there for others, along with the traditional powerful image, contributes profoundly to God's inexpressible greatness. And this compassion is not just for our neighbors and coworkers, but for all peoples. Vajra Ma said, "Motherhood knows no borders, it transcends nations, races, and religions."[148] Jennifer Woolger is in agreement when she says:

> A return to matriarchal consciousness entails honoring the Goddess beneath, above, and around us, as earth, as creation, as life itself. It means a harmonious sharing of power for the benefit of the whole. It means an attitude of celebration of life in its infinite variety.[149]

As women become valued for their wisdom and ability, their confidence in their insightfulness will grow, enabling them to flourish in their model role. Their inclusive outlook will not allow them to judge and oppress others for personal gain, so society will effortlessly shift to a higher consciousness. Maternal love wants to restore all human relationships into wholesome ones, reorder economies, preserve resources, and ban whatever damages the creation. Since the instinctive advice given by women clearly benefits society, men will look to them for advice. As William Bond and Pamela Suffield acknowledge, "Men can respect and follow the guidance of women who have the inner connection to the Great Mother."[150]

Women have a unique function to represent Mother God on earth. It is a hidden gift that more and more women are becoming conscious of. Once women are connected to Mother God, they become truly remarkable because they can substantially help others and themselves. Women's natural closeness and resemblance to Mother God links them to the infinite source of love and wisdom. William Bond and Pamela Suffield honors this when they write, "Women call on the wisdom of the Great Mother to bear children, to rear them, to look after their husbands, and to keep the whole society functioning."[151] They further argues:

Women's link to the Great Mother cannot be totally suppressed. Although they may initially punish men for their behavior, once they are ready to forgive, they will desire to rule by consent. Only in this way can they feel at ease with a leading role in society. When men see that no force will be used, and that women truly desire harmony, not domination, they will become passive and willing to surrender.[152]

While men often seek glory as heroes, women's impact on the world has been quiet and unadorned. It has been like a hidden stream flowing beneath the surface of what happens, just waiting to be discovered. With little fanfare, women have led the evolutionary pathway for humanity with their subtle yet sophisticated calibrator of reality. In fact, feminine power embodied in the motherhood of woman has clearly been the foundation for all cultures. "The psychological and spiritual needs of humanity throughout the ages reflect the need to worship a maternal figure."[153] According to a recent publication from the Institute of Inclusive Security:

Women promote dialogue and build trust. They consistently bridge divides and build coalitions for peace. Whether preventing conflict, contributing to peace processes, or rebuilding their societies after war, women take an inclusive approach. With their collaborative responses to preventing conflict, making peace, and rebuilding societies, women consistently address this cause of conflict and instability, helping to ensure that peace will last.[154]

To come to the point, the Motherhood of God symbolizes our best hope for a viable, sustainable future. In fact, the souls of women and men need Mother God to complete their lives. This is because She represents a solution or antidote to the imbalances that so grievously plague our world. Mother God helps to co-create the harmonious interrelationships needed for balance, as opposed to a hierarchy of power where might is right, and words of terror outweigh words of love. "The Goddess is a powerful catalyst to trigger whatever changes that are needed. Her feminine sacredness counters the flaws in an overly masculine culture by balancing the genders of all races throughout the world."[155] Carol Ochs speaks to the problem plainly. Unless we can envision Father and Mother God as one, there will always be problems. She sums it up by saying:

> Is God male, female, both, neither, other? And what is our relationship with God? The happy solution would be to combine the experiences of matriarchy and patriarchy and see God as both female and male.[156]

Discreetly, throughout history, Mother God has been the champion and companion of the oppressed, particularly women. Mother God has sovereign power that protects, heals, and liberates, thus shaping a new understanding of divine reality. Traditionally, the religious image of divine wrath discloses God's outrage at the harm done to those She loves. She is behind anyone who courageously engages injustice and against whoever harms Her children. Accordingly, women ablaze with righteous anger offer an excellent image of God's indignant power of wrath kindled by injustice. "Perhaps some day women will be able to celebrate themselves openly as female representations of the Almighty God."[157] Andrew Harvey envisions the Mother and Father as already one, and like Shiva and Parvati in Indic lore, eternally united, entwined in love.

> The mythology of tradition restores the image of the sacred marriage in the union of the Divine Father-Mother in the ground of being. There is not a Mother and a Father but the Mother-Father who are one in their eternal embrace; one in their ground, one in their emanation, one in their ecstatic and continuous act of creation through all the invisible dimensions that bring into being and sustain.[158]

The Divine Feminine is the spiritual starting point that encompasses the concepts of wisdom, compassion, and unconditional love, a perfect role model and source of strength for women, and for men as well. It is a principle that looks at things both short term and long term and embraces ancient and new concepts. It is at the root of the equilibrium between the spiritual and pragmatic sides of our lives, which women today are being called upon to revive, as times change. The harmony of the Divine Father-Mother opens hearts and minds to a new understanding of life. Great hope and healing will follow when the meaning of the sacred marriage of Heavenly Father and Heavenly Mother becomes fully conscious in the human soul, and it will inspire more powerful relationships and marriages the world over.

We tend to look for God in the wrong directions. When out of touch with divine intelligence, our minds tend to become narrow and rigid. But if our vision is aligned with truth, we will know it, for our thoughts and prayers will resonate with the universe. Mother God, together with Father God, provide the balance needed for creativity and happiness. Taking time to sit in silence and commune with our divine gender-balanced Parents will bring about a flow of consciousness that will open the floodgates of ideas and solutions that we seek, all grounded in the aesthetic principles of harmony and beauty. As Reverend

Jann Aldredge-Clanton writes, "We are constantly being birthed anew by the Divine Mother/Father, the Creator who keeps on creating and who calls us, in like fashion, to renew and re-envision."[159] Who could ask for a better teacher?

Chapter 6
Testimonies about Mother God

The Mother is supreme reality. She is light itself. Transcendent. It is by Her and through Her that all things moving and motionless shine. It is by the light of her, the Divine, that all things manifest.[160] - **Sondra Ray**

The will in Her works is scrupulous, unsleeping, indefatigable; leaning over us she notes and touches every little detail, finds out every minute defect, gap, twist, or incompleteness, considers and weighs accurately all that has been done and all that remains still to be done hereafter. Nothing is too small or apparently trivial for Her attention; nothing however impalpable or disguised or latent can escape her.[161]
- Sri Aurobindo

The experience of the Mother, of the mother aspect of the godhead, of the motherhood of God, is an immense, constantly expanding experience of the presence of calm power and blissful unconditional love as the ground of all being. That is the presence of the Mother. That is the essential experience that we must all ask for now, whatever our creed or caste or color.[162]
- Andrew Harvey

The universal Mother works out whatever is transmitted by Her transcendent

consciousness from the Supreme and enters into the world She has made. Her presence fills and supports them with the divine spirit and the divine all-sustaining force and delight without which they could not exist.[163]
- **Robert Powell**

The mind of the Great Mother is completely unlimited and can accommodate all ideas and all people, without fear. She has given us parts of Her wisdom and everyone has access to this.[164]
- **William Bond and Pamela Suffield**

The Divine Mother unifies and diversifies. She is the one in the unfolded universe and the universe is the one in her. She is the one who perfects science, the Great Inspiratrix who gives the lift of knowledge to the minds of leading scientists. She is the origin of consciousness, of all the elements, of all the laws of physics, mathematics, music, economics, and languages. She is the primordial cause of all existence and is eternally one with the Father.[165] - **Sondra Ray**

Her spirit is timeless, Her vision and will are high and far-reaching like the flight of an eagle, Her feet are rapid on the upward way and Her hands are outstretched to strike and to support. For She too is the Mother and Her love is as intense as Her wrath and She has a deep and passionate kindness.[166] - **Sri Aurobindo**

The Mother is the worker. She is about creating, laboring, and birthing, and then caring for and providing for Her creations. She takes care of individuals, providing unconditional love, support, and nurturing. She has no boundaries. She loves and accepts all just as they are.[167]
- **Rev. Dr. Karen Tate**

The qualities associated with the Great Mother include maternal solicitude and sympathy, the magic authority of the female, the wisdom and spiritual exaltation that transcend reason; any helpful instinct or impulse; all that is benign, all that cherishes and sustains, that fosters growth and fertility. The place of magic transformation and rebirth, together with the underworld and its inhabitants, are presided over by the mother.[168]
- **Joan Chamberlain Engelsman**

This Mother of the World, the Tao, is the elusive, invisible, inaudible, unfathomable which embraces both forms and formless. It is all-pervading, all-embracing, everywhere, and all things. In birth all things emerge from it. In death they return to it.[169] - **Shirley Nicholson**

The Divine Mother will bring us to the nurturing, tender aspects of ourselves, which are so needed to solve the problems in the world today. The Divine Mother will give us the solutions to our personal problems and to our planetary problems. We need to let Her teach us now.[170]
- **Sondra Ray**

The Mother of the World is the Void, the Inexpressible, the Goddess – whatever name you give to it; it is the light itself. Coming to know that light, you come to know that you are a child of that light.[171] - **Andrew Harvey**

She is the Universal Mother, "my Mother," as Ramakrishna would say, the All-Powerful, who reveals Herself to Her children under different aspects and Divine Incarnations, the Visible God, who leads the elect to the Invisible Reality; and if it so pleases Her, She takes away the last trace of ego from created beings and merges it in the consciousness of the Absolute, the undifferentiated God.[172]
- **Jennifer Barker Woolger**

The Gnostics held the heavenly Feminine Spirit in high regard, naming Her Sophia, or Lady Wisdom. Sophia is the Wisdom of God, a divine Feminine Spirit pervading all of life. She partakes of the power of the Creator, is capable of doing all things, and is regarded as the mother of the gifts of wisdom and prophecy. She is creator, wisdom, and teacher, wise in the ways of humanity, nature, and divinity. In certain mystical traditions she is the consort of God and the lover and inspiration of the wise.[173]
- **Cathy Pagano**

Holy Sophia is coming. She will shine through the darkness and touch the hearts of those who are able to remain free. She will come in Her glory, in Her resplendent beauty, with all Her wisdom and

Her unchanging, everlasting purity.[174] – **Robert Powell and Estelle Isaacson**

Sophia is the companion of every soul. She descends in order to have the initiation of human existence. She shares in our work, She is a teacher of primal playfulness and creativity. We all bear Her seal and signature, not as Her possessions but as sharers in the prima materia of DNA itself.[175] - **Caitlin Matthews**

The Goddess is much more than a traditional Mother of God, or Mother of all the gods, as she was perceived in antiquity. She is not only Mother Nature, and the Mother Earth to whom we owe our being; She is also a spirit that each woman finds within herself and identifies as Her own femaleness. The Goddess may not be transcendent, but She is the most meaningful metaphor for the life force that animates every creature on the planet.[176] - **Barbara Walker**

The Mother gives herself to create this entire universe. She gives herself. Who do you think is suffering in the death of every child from AIDS? The Mother is suffering. She's suffering with no hideaway, with no consolation, because she's not closed and dead as we are. She suffers in every pain just as she delights in every kind of bliss. She is all things and she has no mask and no drug of forgetfulness and no evasion because she has nowhere to run from herself. So she boils and screams and dies within herself, just as she lies peacefully at the bottom of the sea beyond all catastrophes. Everything goes on in her.[177] - **Andrew Harvey**

Every being, every blade of grass, every stone, bug, tree and animal is nothing other than the Mother in disguise. In the language of the Goddess, all of nature was part of Her body and symbolic of Her power.[178] - **Carol P. Christ**

God is the universe. We are all now living inside the body of God. There is nowhere to go to get there, we are already there. There is nowhere to go to get outside of God; there is just a forgetting of this truth. It is impossible not be to be living, right now and always, within God's body. It is only possible to be aware, or unaware, of this fact.[179] - **Monica Sjoo and Barbara Mor**

She watches over all people and all things in heaven and on earth, being of such radiance and brightness that, for the measureless splendor that shines in Her, you cannot gaze on Her face or the garment she wears. For She is awesome in terror and the Thunderer's lightning, and gentle in goodness as the sunshine. Hence, in Her terror and Her gentleness, She is incomprehensible to mortals, because of the dread radiance of divinity in Her face and the brightness that dwells in Her as the robe of Her beauty. She is like the sun, which none can contemplate in its blazing face or in the glorious garment of its rays. For She is with all and in all, and of beauty so great in Her mystery that no one could know how sweetly She bears with people, and what unfathomable mercy She spares them. - **Barbara Newman**

She is coming back into our consciousness through prophecy and visions. She is bringing a profound nurturing, a depth of compassion, and a kind of love we no longer remember, but which was strong in ancient times. This pure feminine energy will awaken in men as well as women, though a story we already know in our hearts once we hear it. The return of the Grandmother has been foretold for hundreds of years.[180] - **Carol Schaefer**

She changes everything she touches and everything she touches, changes.[181]
- **Hallie Iglehart Austen**

She is the creative force of the universe, and the creative force within each of us.[182] - **Teri Degler**

The feminine principle has been recognized by humanity in various aspects. In times long past we have paid her homage as the source of life, the sustainer, the healer, the enlightener, the one who receives in death, and the giver of immortality. She has been the protector of love, the image of beauty, and the object of desire.[183]
- **Shirley Nicholson**

In the Gospel of Mary Magdalene, Mary teaches there is not knowledge of the Father apart from the Mother. One who knows the Mother is near to the Father, but one who denies the Mother is

far from the Father. There is not two, but only one God, and God is both Father and Mother.[184]
- **Tricia McCannon**

Sophia, clothed in radiant rose-hued light, arose from Her throne. Her beauty was ineffable. Rosy light and harmonies and fragrances emanated from Her Being. Astonished and humbled by Her infinite love for humanity, I yearned to feel the same love.[185]
- **Robert Powell and Estelle Isaacson**

Mother God's spirit is: intelligent, holy, unique, manifold, subtle, mobile, clear, unpolluted, distinct, invulnerable, loving, keen, irresistible, beneficent, humane, steadfast, sure, free from anxiety, all-powerful, overseeing all, and penetrating through all spirits that are intelligent, pure, and most subtle.[186]
- **Asphodel P. Long**

The Mother is all-willing, all-loving, all-powerful, at once the ground, energy, and the goal of evolution. There is no end or limit imaginable to Her love or its transforming powers. In Her and in our working consciously, directly, and humbly with Her is our great human hope.[187]
- **Andrew Harvey**

Four great aspects of the Mother, four of Her leading powers and personalities have stood in front of Her guidance of this universe and in Her dealings with the terrestrial play. One is Her personality of calm wideness, comprehending wisdom, tranquil benignity, inexhaustible compassion, sovereign and surpassing majesty, and all-ruling greatness. Another embodies Her power of splendid strength and irresistible passion, Her warrior mood, Her overwhelming will, Her impetuousness, swiftness, and world-shaking force. A third is vivid and sweet and wonderful, with Her deep secret beauty and harmony and fine rhythm, Her intricate and subtle opulence, Her compelling attraction and captivating grace. The fourth is equipped with Her close and profound capacity of intimate knowledge, careful flawless work, and quiet and exact perfection of all things. Wisdom, Strength, Harmony, and Perfection are their attributes and it is these powers that they bring with them to the world.[188] - **Sri Aurobindo**

The gifts of the goddess are wisdom, knowledge, love, peace, curiosity, imagination, art, creativity, and free will, all the feminine virtues that do not produce war, enslavement, and evil.[189]
- **Nancy Oakes**

She will bring together and unify hearts. Each heart is a part of the whole. To live in the embrace of Sophia is to feel one's self as part of the whole. It is to know one's self as Her beloved creation and to see all people as Her begotten. She is the great unifier. She will reveal the jewels of truth, beauty, and goodness that are present in every person, culture, and religion.[190]
- **Robert Powell and Estelle Isaacson**

The Great Mother is not only the parent of the gods but also of all creation. She is particularly identified with the welfare of animals and humans and with the Earth itself. She is a source of healing and renewal. She is named 'great parent of all nature' rather than Nature, and in this respect resembles Wisdom as creator who brought all into being.[191] - **Asphodel P. Long**

She never forsakes Her place on Earth or with Her children. She weeps with us when we are banished from Eden and from our homelands; She wanders with us in our long exile, and She wails with us in our grief. But as the immanence of the Divine, She remains steadfastly with us, waiting for us to bring the divine union within ourselves so that She too can be wholly united with the Divine. Thus She is truly God with us. She is the mother of the world, the embodiment of the Divine, and the living heart of God that beats within us and gives us life.[192] - **Teri Degler**

It is Sophia who opens up to us the mysteries of the seasons, of the relationships between Earth and the cosmos, the healing properties of plants and the mysteries of the animal kingdom, and the true relationship between humanity and the animal, plant, and mineral kingdoms. It is Sophia who reveals to us the properties of the different precious stones, what they convey to us, and their healing powers. Sophia reveals herself to any human being who upholds the path of justice and righteousness. From age to age, Sophia enters into holy souls and all those who seek her.[193]
- **Robert Powell**

Sophia offers many gifts and many resources we can draw on. One is Her faithfulness. She won't give up on us. She won't go away, even when we ignore her. She won't disappear, even when our old scriptures write Her out. She'll be there for us when we ask Her to be present.[194]

- **Karen Speestra**

Sophia is the great lost Goddess who has remained intransigently within orthodox spiritualties. She is veiled, blackened, denigrated, and ignored most of the time, or else She is exalted, hymned, and pedestalled as an allegorical abstraction of female divinity. She is allowed to be a messenger, a mediator, a helper, a handmaid; She is allowed to be seen in charge, fully self-possessed and creatively operative.[195]

- **Caitlin Matthews**

Sophia permeates the ground of existence. She is the spiritual essence within all matters. She embodies the wisdom of creation and bears the presence of the Divine into human souls and communities as the agent of spiritual love and inspiration.[196]

- **Robert Powell and Estelle Isaacson**

Spirit-Sophia is the source of transforming energy among all creatures. She initiates novelty, instigates change, transforms what is dead into new stretches of life. Fertility is intimately related to Her re-creative power, as is the attractiveness of sex. It is she who is ultimately playful, fascinating, pure, and wise, luring human beings into the depths of love. As mover and encourager of what tends towards stasis, Spirit-Sophia inspires human creativity and joy in the struggle. Wherever the gift of healing and liberation in however partial a manner reaches the winterized or damaged Earth, or peoples crushed by war and injustice, or individual persons weary, harmed, sick, or lost on life's journey, there the new creation in the Spirit is happening.[197] - **Elizabeth A. Johnson**

Underlying every aspect of Sophia is Her unconditional love. We don't need do anything – *nothing* – and she will still welcome us 'home', just as we are. By Her example, she teaches us how to love each other.[198] - **Karen Speestra**

The Queen of Heaven and the Mother of the Earth has been forgotten by Her children, dishonored, and mistreated. It is time we honor Her.[199] - **Tricia McCannon**

The Queen creates a sense of order, safety, and a feeling that the future is secure. It is the Queen in woman who is the architect of the good life for all. The Queen solves everything. With her, life is "as it was always meant to be."[200]
- **Rev. Dr. Karen Tate**

The Universe Mother Spirit never ceases creative activity in a growing and perfecting universe.[201]
- **The Urantia Book**

The energy that flows from the heart is a feminine energy. It is a very powerful loving energy guiding our thoughts to what is the universal truth.[202] - **Nancy Oakes**

The temple of Sophia is not the sanctuary of just one religion. The temple of Sophia embraces all benevolent spiritual traditions. Sophia does not pick and choose, and weigh one tradition against the others. She embraces all and will hold all in the circle of Her Love until all is One.[203]
- **Robert Powell and Estelle Isaacson**

She is the beauty of the green earth, the life-giving waters, the consuming fire, the radiant moon, and the fiery sun. She is the Star Goddess and Spiderwoman; she weaves the luminous web that creates the universe. As earth, the great planetary Spirit-Being, She germinates life within Her dark womb.[204]
- **Monica Sjoo and Barbara Mor**

The Spirit is the life of the life of all creatures; the way in which everything is penetrated with connectedness; a burning fire who sparks, ignites, inflames, kindles hearts; a guide in the fog; a balm for all wounds; a shining serenity; an overflowing fountain that spreads to all sides. She is life, movement, color, radiance, restorative stillness in the din. Her power makes all withered sticks and souls green again with the juice of life. She purifies, absolves, strengthens, heals, gathers the perplexed, seeks the lost. She pours the juice of contrition into hardened hearts. She plays music in the soul, being herself the melody of praise and joy. She awakens mighty hope, blowing everywhere the winds of renewal in creation. - **Hildegard of Bingen**

In the midst of agony, Spirit-Sophia who loves people teaches the ways of justice and courage.[205]
- **Elizabeth A. Johnson**

Sophia is the grand root of the synthesis of everything that is created, that is, the entire creation and not just all creatures.[206]
- **Robert Powell and Estelle Isaacson**

In India, the supreme being has *never* been worshipped exclusively in a masculine form. The supreme being is also worshipped as the Goddess in Her many aspects. She is, for example, worshipped as Sarasvati, the Goddess of wisdom and learning; she is worshipped as Lakshmi, the Goddess of prosperity; and Santana Lakshmi, the Goddess who gives new life within a woman. She is also worshipped as Durga, the Goddess of strength and power. There was a time when men revered women as the embodiment of these very qualities. She was considered an extension of the Goddess, and a manifestation of Her attributes on Earth.[207]
- **Sondra Ray**

And a great sign appeared in heaven, a woman robed with the sun, beneath Her feet the moon and on Her head a crown of twelve stars.[208]
- **The Book of Revelation 12:1**

To me the Goddess is the feeling I have when I'm troubled or confused and I keep quiet for a

minute and then another voice comes into me. It's my own voice, but I feel like it's also another. It guides me. It gives me some specific action to take. That's my personal understanding of the Goddess. The voice is always female and totally loving, warm, caring, and understanding – motherly, sisterly. Whenever I feel hopeless about this world, it comforts me.[209]
- **Barbara Walker**

If you focus on the Goddess, it is almost as if she begins to notice you and takes you under Her wing. She gradually begins to reveal herself in all Her complexity, and sometimes in unexpected ways. This is an ongoing process, spiraling to deeper and deeper levels, always continuing. As you allow the Goddess to become part of your daily life, you will become more and more able to embody the Sacred Feminine and complete your whole self.[210] - **Hallie Iglehart Austen**

I saw and met a divine presence that was toweringly female yet beyond sexuality; She was arresting and awe-inspiring. There was the impression of a great dark mask covering what was not a face. Above the mask of the face-not-a-face was an impression of hair, sweeping upwards and outwards on either side, becoming great wings, as of an eagle facing me, poised to soar upwards or beat downwards in bone-breaking fury. The hair becoming wings was not joined to the mask, but above and close to it. Between the wings was neither shape nor form, but a dark purple fire. The presence came unasked, an encounter with the whole being of

the one God, known in that moment as She. It was as if the complex diamond of the divine shone at me intensely from that one facet.[211]
- **Paul R. Smith**

I was looking down on all this, when suddenly I felt a 'presence.' It seemed very ancient and wise and definitely female. I can't describe it any closer than that, but I felt that this presence, this being, was looking down on me, on this church and these people and saying, 'The poor little ones! They mean so well and they understand so little.' I felt whoever 'she' was, she was incredibly old and patient; she was exasperated with the way things were going on the planet but she hadn't given up hope that we would start making some sense of the world. So, after that, I knew I had to find out more about her. - **Alison Harlow**

It never occurred to me that God was female. Discovering that femaleness gave me a tremendous sense of relief. I felt Her blessing touch me for the first time. I felt a great weight drop from me. I could actually feel my last prejudices against my own female mind and body falling away.[212] - **Margot Adler**

Mother God is very righteous, and if you call on Her when you're in danger of dark entities She wields Her sword to dispel them. She has also been known to help get rid of physical and chemical addictions by wielding Her sword to cut away the need for alcohol, drugs, and other addictive substances. And you can ask Her to intervene when you're worried about your family, friends, or spouse.[213] - **Sylvia Browne**

My personal vision of God the mother incarnated in my mother and Her mother gave me, from childhood, the clearest certainty of woman as the truer image of Divine Spirit. Because she was a force living within me, she was more real, more powerful than the remote Fathergod. I believe in Her because I experienced her.[214]
- **Susanne Schaup**

She knows when I need Her and She responds without being asked. She calms me when I get frustrated if things are not going just right and when I have a decision to make or I'm wrestling with a problem. She helps me rationalize each situation to its best result. I'm so happy that She has taken my hand and is walking step by step with me.[215] - **Sylvia Browne**

Sophia appeared to me in the figure of a woman with a very friendly and dignified demeanor. Her countenance radiated like the sun and She was dressed in a garment of translucent gold.[216]
- **Thomas Schipflinger**

It's very important to me to have a being to whom I can turn to when things are hard, to whom I can return thanks when things are good, who is a greater source of knowledge than I am, from whom I can learn, and who loves me – which is not to say She doesn't love everyone else, but She has to love me personally – and

who I feel is trustworthy and powerful. [217]
- **Barbara Walker**

When I feel weak, the Goddess is someone who can help and protect me. When I feel strong, She is the symbol of my own power. At other times, I feel Her as the natural energy in my body and the world.[218] - **Carol P. Christ**

I was shown two chairs. On the one closest to me sat a woman; next to Her on Her right sat a man. I knew that the woman represented Heavenly Mother; the man represented Heavenly Father. Heavenly Mother did the talking. "Ron, first I want you to know that even though you see two here, I am only one. I am only one. The reason I am manifesting to you as your Divine Mother is because it is most appropriate for me to come to you this way because of where you are right now in your spiritual growth." She invited me to come and sit on Her lap. I took the form and position of a child and did so. "I want you to spend a lot of time right here during this period. I am healing you of certain wounds that you still possess from your childhood."[219] - **Ron Pappalardo**

Years ago, I had a direct experience with God as Mother and Father. This experience occurred at a time of great personal distress in which I needed an absolute answer about my future. My desperate prayer seemed to open up the spiritual world and even as I fell into a semi-dreamlike state, I felt my spirit exit through the top of my head. I entered into a place that was ethereal, my surroundings were white like clouds and there was nothing that was substantial. I knew I was not on an earthly plane. A woman appeared and began drawing close to me. She was statuesque, dressed in a full-length, shimmery robe of some kind, and had long dark hair. I do not recall Her face other than it was kindly and feminine. As she came closer to me, I came closer to her. After a short time, she started becoming larger and she gathered me into Her arms, as if I was a baby. I then realized she was baring Her breast to nurse me and I remember thinking to myself, "How can this be? I am a full-grown woman!" But I didn't resist Her at all, and during the nursing experience, I felt a stream of life-giving nourishment, a warming energy of love flow into me and through me until it reached my toes. It was rapturous. - **Anonymous**

I will never forget the first time Mother and Father God came to me in meditation. They came to me because I asked them to. Mother God came first and then Father God came to me. I have never had such an outpouring of emotion in this lifetime. My body was shaking uncontrollably and tears were streaming down my face. The energy and the love that I felt from them cannot be described. Mother and Father God told me that they don't want to be worshiped, they simply want us to know them, they want us to know and feel the love they have for us, and they want us to love ourselves and all living things. For love is who we truly are. – **Anonymous**

Chapter 7
In Her Own Words

Very few of you know me, so I need to start by introducing myself. You know of the Great Father/God/Allah/Creator – choose your term – but not truly about me, the Great Mother. I've been mostly shunted to the side for several thousand years, and it's time for me to be recognized as much as the Great Father. Most of you were not raised with much awareness, if any, of me. I am the feminine aspect of the Great Mystery. Your religions have taught you about God, Allah, Yahweh, etcetera, as the Creator Father, but there has been minimal discussion about me, the Great Divine Compassionate Mother, in your places of worship for many, many centuries. I am as difficult to define as the Great Mystery or God. I am the Creatrix. I am the Great Goddess. I am beyond description, beyond understanding, beyond religion, beyond dogma. I am. Yet that is challenging for you humans to grasp since most of you need something more tangible to help you understand. Perhaps if you perceived me as the greatest Mother figure you've ever experienced, of compassion, gentleness, and love exponential, then you would begin to understand. But I am far more than that, as I am beyond your limited human concepts. My energy swirls in every single thing in the universe, in dynamic balance with the sacred masculine energies. I am embodied here on Earth within the powerful consciousness of our Planetary Caretaker, Earth Mother. Your planet has a spiritual consciousness and there are those who can listen to her. In balance with the Great Father, I am the procreative force that birthed all of you into existence – including all the four-leggeds, winged ones, finned ones and more – through Earth Mother. The full evolution of stunning biodiversity, energy dances, water cycles, and breathtaking flowers and so much more source from my and Creator's love. I am also embodied in all life on Earth, in all women and men, stones, insects, trees, all matter on your planet. My energy dances in the very atoms of your cells as part of the Great Mystery and sacredness of life. Your bodies are made up of the sacred minerals, water, nutrients, and energies that pulse, cycle, and move over Earth Mother's skin. I am there in all. I am the Great Mother force that can be gentle as a morning mist, whose capacity for forgiveness, softness, and procreativity are huge, absolutely huge. Or I can rage like a flood-swollen river. I am the Sacred Feminine force. I am within the One.[220] – *The Great Mother Bible by Mare Cromwell*

I am Nature, the universal Mother, mistress of the elements, primordial child of time, sovereign of all things spiritual, queen of the dead, queen also of the immortals, the single manifestation of all gods and goddesses that are. My nod governs the shining lights of Heaven, the wholesome sea breezes, and the lamentable silences of the world below. Though I am worshiped in many aspects, known by countless names and propitiated with all manner of different rites, yet the whole round Earth venerates me.[221] – **When God Was a Woman by Merlin Stone**

I am the Mother Reality from which all levels of consciousness are born, including the subtle realm. I am the one called Shakti, the creative energy and power which births all manifestations, all worlds, all universes.[222]
– *Conversations with the Goddess by Dorothy Atalla*

I am the Mother. I am both transcendent and immanent, source and all that streams from it. I am one with all things in creation and one in boundless light within and beyond it. Adore every being and thing, from the whale to the ladybug, as life of my life. Honor yourself humbly as my divine child, and see, know, and celebrate all other beings as my divine children. Whatever you do to or for anyone, you do to or for me. I and you and nature are one love, one glory; protecting nature is protecting yourselves. Dissolve forever all schisms and separations between sects and religions. Know that there are as many paths as there are people. Unlearn all the "religious" propaganda that tries to tell you that you need intermediaries in your relationship with me. I can be contacted by anyone, anywhere, at any time and in any circumstance, simply by saying my name, however you image it. Know that my revelation is a revolution, a revolution that demands calmly a transformation of all the terms and conditions of life on earth.

Remember always there is no Mother without the Father, no Goddess without God.[223] - *The Return of the Mother by Andrew Harvey*

I am the doorway of eternity, the White Dove of hope that enters every age as a promise of that which can be. I am the dreams of the holy and the vision of men of reason. I am the she who is always present – waiting endlessly, loving endlessly, hoping endlessly that my children will awaken.[224] - *She Who Is Always Present by Tricia McCannon*

I give the Milk of Divine Grace and the Honey of Eternal Love to all those who seek my face. I bless you with My Grace and the sweetness of My love. I hold you to My breast and nurture you with My love. I have heard your entreaties; you have cried to be held by your Mother; and I have heard your cries through the ages and lifetimes. How I have ached to hold you and to bring you out of the desolate places in which you have been wandering; for I have watched you wander in the fallen world amongst thorns and thistles.[225] - *The Mystery of Sophia by Robert Powell and Estelle Isaacson*

I am the beauty running through the world, to make it associate in ordered groups, the ideal held up before the world to make it ascend. I am the Eternal Feminine. I was the bond that held the foundations of the universe. I extend my being into the soul of the world. I am the magnetic force of the universal presence and the ceaseless ripple of its smile. I open the door to the whole heart of creation. In me, the soul is at work to sublimate the body – grace to divinize the soul.[226] - *The Mystery of Sophia by Robert Powell and Estelle Isaacson*

As women go into Myself through their own inner journeys, they will discover – not just intellectually but at the depths of their spirit – their true feminine nature. They will not need validation by men because they will know not only their own worth but also their own oneness with me. This is a power that can never be diminished by rejection by men nor can it be augmented by men's attraction to them. Women will learn to respond to the masculine with the fullness of their own being as females.[227] – *Conversations with the Goddess by Dorothy Atalla*

There are centuries and centuries of woundedness on the part of both women and men because you humans have lost the balance between the masculine and the feminine. This was lost when you lost your sacred connection to me, Mother God. I would like to see all women heal and find their voices and their womb-wisdom along with their feminine power based in the very center of their being. I would like to see all men heal from the repressed ways they have been taught and heal their wounded hearts. I would like to see all religions and belief systems speak to the balance between the Sacred Feminine and the Divine Masculine.[228] – *The Great Mother Bible by Mare Cromwell*

If you seek me with true desire for knowledge,
I shall be with you.
I am the seed and the source of your visible world.
I am the ocean of light in which your soul lives.
I am the ruler of space.
I am the creator of cycles of time.
Fire, air, light, water, and earth obey me.
Feel me as the spiritual origin of all matter.[229]
- *The Sophia Teachings by Robert Powell*

I am the creation from the beginning.
Everything in the creation is me.
All creation is growing toward me.
It is begun in ecstasy.
It is continued in ecstasy.
It is sustained in ecstasy.
I will expand in ecstasy.[230]
   - *The Return of the Mother by Andrew Harvey*

Chapter 8
Messages from Mother God
via C.K.

I want something different, and frankly, it would be rude of Me in My relationship with humanity to say nothing. I am not that kind of woman. I am not that kind of man. I am not that kind of God or Being. I treasure love, but I also want to be involved with it. To say otherwise is to lie, and a lie is hardly the truest of loves. I am with you, and for it to work for all we need our truest love. Once we gain it, we do not lose it. It belongs to us forever, eternally. We still, however, have to gain it.

When I created the universe, I wanted to experience happiness and love. I wanted to embrace love. Yet most men and women have never heard of Heavenly Mother. She is not well-known. Yet, Mother God has never forsaken Her original design. I want to make it perfectly clear that My original goals are not flawed. I want to make it equally clear that men and women are equal in my sight.

All around the world, women have to develop faith in Heavenly Mother, believing the unbelievable. Holding on for dear life to Her hand, Her astute character, Her mind-boggling image. Please give men a chance to know God through women and whatever you do, give God a chance to know each human being completely. Please accept My advantage in knowing all gender realities. Leave Mother God out and I am half a God, a struggling, solo parent. Why not let God in the Feminine directly support women? My point is: call Heavenly Parent, call on Me when you need Me fully functioning as a capable Mother. We want to build something real here. You need all aspects of God. I am looking forward to all people starting to develop their faith in the femininity of God.

When God designed humanity, She/He had a vision. God created the universe to experience happiness and to embrace love. God is working to see happy families. I still have the conviction that someday I will see it. Surely, God had and still has a feminine perspective in creating. The central heart and hope of Mother God is to create the circumstance where men and women can fulfill the purpose of creation.

My real problem has been the heartache of separation and the terrible loss and pain in lives spent in unhappiness, without resolution, with limited growth, and with only a handful of people informed enough about how to care for others. Learn to understand why God chose to invest in replicating Her Feminine self and His Masculine self. We need an age for women because women deserve to receive absolute love, to have a way to attain, maintain, and to liaise with God without fear. Such women can face anything.

Human beings have to break past habit and come to terms with the true identity of God.

They have to learn a new tradition of trusting, even unconditionally, a Divine Mother. Everyone knows that the advice provided by their father does not always agree with their mother's. This lack of uniformity in a father and mother's advice is not an act of terror on God's part, but a gift of heart, love, character, and self.

Historians have their theories for why things went wrong. For Me, as Creator, it is a simple yet terrible fact: God, in humanity, was under-resourced. Has humanity noticed the complete and comprehensive hands of Mother God? Just understand this: humanity has to go further. Women across the globe must be free. Mother God expects us to consider, move, act, give, and invest to make a difference. The creation was designed for comprehensive use. I envisage a world where no one would want. All forms of expression would be owned by God. We need fulfillment. We need to start empowering women so they can solve problems, just like men.

Anytime God spoke in history, God encountered skeptics. At what stage or stages can they be found? They can be found at all stages. Those who are far advanced know that skepticism is a gift of God, a diamond in the rough. I am not trying to instruct humanity so that people would not question Me. However, if God is to introduce a greater working for unpacking the meaning of "Heavenly Parent," wouldn't you think that God would know that

God would face skeptics? Did you know I am happy to face them and welcome them with loving parental arms? Skeptics are not the last sheep to be found; they are often among the first to be found.

We have to build an ideal world, and to do it you have to manage skepticism. Healthy skepticism can help anyone be successful. There is not a human being alive who does not need to hear the word "no." I wish you all well and I know that there will be skeptics. Bring it on! I also have masculinity and can out-muscle anyone, but what I really want is process-oriented delivery. I want women to have a say in processes. Is that unreasonable?

Skepticism is not difficult for Me. It is lack of respect that is problematic. But if you have not learned humility, where will God turn to teach you? I am afraid it will or would have to be Plan B. If Plan A doesn't bring the ideal, we'll keep trying. Most of you continually check in with God during your lives. Thank you. It means a lot to Me. So much. You may never know.

Do you know the simplest way to know if what you are doing is good? Just ask yourself, "Is it beautiful?" or, "What aspects of it are beautiful?" From now on, just ask yourself, is it beautiful? For example, I offered my hand, in a handshake, to him: was it beautiful? I kissed my spouse goodnight: was it beautiful? I offered constructive criticism: was it, or what aspects of it, was beautiful? Isn't it about time we focus on love, spruce up our ability to perceive beauty, and become the kind of people who eternally can appreciate an offering? The implications are that you will have ownership, that you will add something, and that you will offer your hearts. All perfected beings are beautiful. You have to recognize beauty in your own way. Be beautiful, outstanding, amazing. Be loving. Those are things I love.

I accept those who judge Me as a failure, but I Myself do not accept failure as an option, not a permanent option, that is. Failure, like the human body, is passing, and it cannot be eternal. We move from there to other dimensions, aspects, spaces, and places, whether in being or in heart or otherwise. Then, how can failure be permanent? So we make life more enjoyable by giving, but don't think for a moment that that excludes laughter or anything else.

I am tired of going it alone, bringing patience into the picture, time and time again. Disappointing responses break my heart. As a Mother, I have had enough of the violence. Surely you can see that. My skirts are torn, my breast bare, and My virtue put to question. Let us live the dream, work for the ideal, and manage violence. We are not the children of God who are to be provoked. We are not lambs to slaughter nor those who throw down our weapons of self-defense. Heavenly Father and I must ascertain our own righteousness. We must not be seen as the Great Being way out in front of our daughters and our sons. No, we, He and I, wish to be close. Decisions regarding the family cannot ignore the female part of the Godhead. I am not a Divine Being who wants to be mocked. You know that. Nobody wants to be mocked. It has to be a quality from God. Similarly, as First Woman, I do not want to be mocked.

I have been reduced to working in extremely limited ways, whereas the creation was designed for comprehensive use. I envisioned a world where no one would want. We would still have the tears. Of course, we would; but we would have investment. Each person without exception would thrive in investment. Everywhere you moved, you would find a person, people, ready, capable, and willing to invest, and each linked to God.

We are like the handicapped children of God. Parents are responsible for what their children do. That is My attitude as Heavenly Parent. My emotions can now flow to women, and women can articulate how their emotions are of God. And if they, in desire, want to be with God, they can further articulate how their emotions are not only of God but one with God in heart, love, gratitude, and any other specified emotion. We no longer have to fear emotions, because God, as co-owner of emotion, can employ acts of referenced love, in emotion, with women. Women will be able to fully share, in written texts, video clips, and in personal sharing how their emotions are of God, how what they are feeling is from God, and how God is with them in emotion.

God is allowed to say what She does not like, just like any man or woman, without fear. Mother God hated the course of history as dictated by men alone. I don't want to be congratulated for pulling humanity out of hell iota by iota, inch by inch, hair by hair. Whose move is it? Whose age is it, women's or men's? But, as you women try to grapple with responsibility, don't call Mother God irresponsible and a product of non-interventionist theory, please.

Generally, people do not communicate effectively about their needs unless there is a willing and capable audience. God isn't any different. The difference is that today we have seen change and there is a new foundation, and this presents room for education and for a new audience. Please consider My needs, as Mother to all. When can God begin on a regular basis to assist humanity, even as a friend? As a helpmate? As a lover? God is much more than a confessor.

Almighty God is strapped and unable to express Herself. Only work can change this. When people really experience Mother God and say Mother God told me, things will change. When you liaise with God, you will get a good outcome. We need to make it applicable to whatever we do.

Men and women are designed to live happily in life, in families, in communities, in societies, spending time with each other and with God. This is why most people want to rely on God as the glue, as there is simply too much information for human beings to manage. My vision extends far into the future, only now it includes women, which is why we can effect change on the global and cosmic levels. The vision must include all and be eternal. The vision must produce results, but women, men, and God, and even children must evaluate those results, given that the purpose of life is to pursue goodness.

God had not set out to make one generation or one gender superior to another. After women are able to liaise directly with God and report to their husbands and other women, we will see for the first time in history a God who is able to pursue Her Original Design; that is, all things original can be communicated to women, making a circumstance on earth for existing human women on the ground to be able to communicate freely with God, without prejudice. In particular, minority women of ethnic origin will be able to find common ground in grasping hold of an Original God Female.

The desire of God is to provide people with the tools they need to face adversity. Those who can undertake to review what has occurred are dear to the Heart of God, for with that, they set themselves out to be available to God, for progress, for building, for creating. We don't get this without reflection. We actually need people to stop and review the past.

When we speak of the need of God, are we talking of an individual being or are we looking more comprehensively at the management of God's expectation in relation to the creation? It is the latter. We would think that before God lifted a finger to create, God would have had plenty of time to manage Her/His own existence and to determine what She/He needed, let alone what was important to Herself/Himself. No mother wants to see her child excluded indefinitely. Let's remember the criteria: Does it meet the needs of all, and is there enough benefit to be recognized by God, humanity, or both?

If God is to be distinct and separate from created beings, God must fulfill minimal requirements. God must manage self, integrity, vision, purpose, needs, and happiness. Ultimately, God can find the most happiness in a conjugal relationship where love is reliable, dependable, and trusted, and where individual needs and God's needs are met. Human beings have needs. We must understand God's needs to build the ideal. God's desire has not been researched.

God must characterize Her concern in all settings, not just in the political backdrop or when politics are front and center. I need a broader base to support humanity. Please support Me across the board in all contexts. I know you know I want to take care of you, but I still need a landing place, a platform, and a way to be with you, to share and to honor in the Feminine. I beg you to join Me and sustain the hope of mankind. Humanity needs love, and I, My children, I need a place to be received broadly. Even the saints in heaven would be inspired. So how valuable is it to broaden our understanding of supporting God? It is invaluable.

What concepts did God wish humanity to come upon? First and foremost, you are My people. You cannot be any other's people because there is no other. We are no longer betrayed by the opposite gender, but we live vibrantly with God, with each other, and in love. So, if love must be creative, good, and holy, how would you rank yourself? Are you creative in moving with God, a living Parent? Is your relationship with God vibrant? Is it set upon the strength of your ancestors, your spouse's ancestors, and upon the strength of God, as well? What are My strengths today if not to express Self in Feminine form too?

May you come to share your love with God, knowing that Whoever I am, I am surely trustworthy. Entrust your questions to God. The position of family is meant to be where love is amplified, complete, reflected, given, shared, understood, and one where God Herself/Himself is lifted up, not to be praised but to experience life, love, joy, character, form, spirit, and joy yet again.

The targeting of women was to allow a degree of control. Women have been raised to call God as "He," potentially not understanding God fully. God is trying to remove the dominance of man. Everybody suffers if things are not in balance. Let's create and use the vocabulary that God has femininity. We should create a divine pronoun of balance. We need it and we don't have it. We need to integrate vocabulary changes into our language. God is a divine being of harmonized masculinity and femininity. New insights of understanding the roles and relationships of Mother God and Father God, especially the nuances of Mother's love and Father's love can be applied toward resolving social, economic, and political issues.

We finally have humanity correctly referring to God in terms of His/Her parental responsibility as Heavenly Parent. Do we yet see the divided masculine and feminine responsibilities of God coming into force in humanity or in the relationship between humanity and the angelic world? Do we see both men and women consulting God over direction and regarding this direction about how to relate to God? We saw that Eve and Adam did not consult with God or with each other before they acted, so how do we expect to break the tradition when the acts we require today are that both men and women consult with God and with each other about their experiences with God? Where are the conferences on the Earth about the nature of God, the identity of God, and the means by which God in the new form of Heavenly Parent relates to humanity?

Chapter 9
Mother God on Femininity
via C.K.

History has been gruesome in that it robbed God of femininity, preventing many women and girls from relating to God in the truest of fashion. Virtues for the average woman can be consulted about with God, in the feminine. Women no longer have to face a blank stare from Mother God. Mother God is fully available to them. The ideal of God, both Feminine and Masculine, speaks to the fact that God, in Her femininity, has been minimized. Heavenly Mother has a reckoning yet to be done, but with a vision eternal for absolute, true, and beautiful love. Fortunately, we will have generations to come, and we will get there.

People did not come to terms with the femininity of God. It was never recorded in the Bible. They did not counter the Our Father as a prayer. People accepted the pronoun He for God without question. A percentage of people understood that at times the pronoun He was transmutable to She. Yet do people understand why God might refer to Herself as She? Femininity is so valuable to God that, of course, God would refer to Herself as a She! So, who are we to become? We are to become the people who liaise with God, in all God's aspects. We are to become the people who live with God, in all God's aspects. We are to become the people who co-design with God, and not just with the Father.

God never lost either femininity or masculinity. Did I misplace My femininity, like an earring, a handbag, or a set of car keys? If it is true that I am One Being, and I Am, I must be able to hold logical conversations with My own children as a Mother. I am here to introduce Myself as a female thinker, a rational being in the feminine. Look at it this way: You like to engage with your favorite subjects, with what you know about, with what you enjoy, and where you can make a difference. Why would Mother God be any different?

Men and women never welcomed Me into the conversation, not in the Feminine. They did not leave the door open or light a candle to allow Me to speak to them. They didn't know it was possible. Their fathers had not told them and their mothers were equally remiss in presenting such a possibility. If women accept that God works laterally through other women, we will have an exciting future, because we will have recognized that God designed the creation to work with. God can work even more effectively through women. We do want real and effective change. It all stands to reason; we must tie into the love of Mother God—not His love only. It seems like we score higher points on referring to Heavenly Father.

As one unified being, I have been waiting for a long time to express femininity. I have been waiting a long time to be recognized, in My Self, as having feminine value, just as humanity has recognized God in My Self as having masculine value, even if it is a diminished understanding.

The ability of God to express Herself is under-researched. In My Femininity, I struggle to feel valuable, because I designed creation and women to express Myself. If women do not express Me, I am lost, unable to be Myself. Like any woman or man, I can retreat, think, work, and plan, but lost engagement is precisely that, lost engagement. Women must engage with God, break the mold that previous women have set up. The image presented of the woman collapsed around the globe does not send a message forth that a woman can be confident in accomplishing a result, unless the result alone is to provide sympathy, love, and relationship, in caring for the downtrodden. That aspect of womanhood is but one aspect of woman, women and femininity. I tell you, in the feminine, I have suffered much. My suffering is only exacerbated if we do nothing to change the future and break the mold.

Men have not seen too that women have a responsibility that is not male in nature. They have not researched the unique responsibility of women. Christianity could not believe that women, who in their eyes were meek and not powerful, could be counted on. Their female shoulders could not handle what God (the He) wanted done. A woman of the past could not be a philosopher unless she was born to a wealthy and affluent family, but a pauper boy could rise to high ranks, i.e., like Jesus. For much of history, men have chosen to bypass God when I showed them femininity or shared My motherly heart with them.

When you see what a good woman has done, you can praise God, knowing that She made that woman. If you praise Me, and you are a man, praise Me for creating women; do not forget to add an element of love: soothing, sympathy, anxiety, worry, hope, passion, joy, admiration, or even ignorance, ignorant bliss. Education will help people make the jump to Mother God, or, if you would, to accessing the mothering qualities of God. My qualities can only become real in relationships, through give and receive action. That is how the creation was made. I am looking for a world where women trust men and men trust women. Let's stop pretending to be men and let the journey of true love and absolute value between God and women begin.

I wonder, rhetorically, if women will take the opportunity to know the female aspects of God, to delight in them, to inform others about them, to take them to the ends of the earth, and now too, to the ends of heaven? Are you the type of woman or man to recognize that this is valuable? Are you the type of person to redefine the Godhead? Or would you leave it to the old scripture writers who left their mark long ago, a mark that still lingers in triggered responses in the here and now? If we recognize God, we will understand that God wants to give in superb feminine ways. She wants to give, to take, to receive, to offer, to provide, to query, to manage, to afford, to secure, and to love. Therefore, God is working furiously to produce better understandings for women, so that they and their brothers might be the ones to recognize God.

When women question everything, they become the owners of love, powerful, beautiful, captivating, and welcomed by all. For generations, the realm of education was denied to girls and women. Very few women in preceding centuries had a chance to ask wide-ranging questions of God, questions about life, questions about the Godhead. As women experience and review the content of their life with God, mutual joy can be guaranteed through their joint participation in life. To me, it's just a matter of how far we get, how fast we travel, move, or consider things.

As anyone might gather, the Godhead, the Creator, must constantly assess Her/His Creation. A woman who does not continually assess the state of the child growing within her would clearly be deficient in love. God developed these and many other processes, yet so many of them are in want of conversations with God. Women's talk shows and women's magazines do not feature women reporting fluid and real conversations with Mother God. I designed women to want to talk, to share, to speak. I designed some women to want to speak flowingly, extensively, and even out of turn. I offer women many opportunities for communication in their lives, and they know how to articulate their experiences. Nevertheless, throughout history, women's experiences are not filled with pure, clear, and extensively understood communication, either from God to women or from women to God. Were any of them recorded, handed down, or well-known in human society? Hence, our society is not overflowing with information about the love of God in the Feminine.

As Creator, as Mother, as Father, I want to pursue the upskilling of all languages. I am interested in parents being able to assist their children in any situation. I am interested in community education. The imperatives for any society must be reviewed by women in order to achieve its utmost at living with God. Respect the right and need of Mother God to work through time for the happiness of all. Celebrate your identity in God, for those who celebrate will bring joy to every aspect of God.

Future female biblical scholars will unpack volumes of information about not only the women in the Bible but the specific communications they had with God, looking at gender, at what was not said, at what did or did not happen, at what could have happened, and, very importantly, at what should have happened. If there had been ample and direct communication between God and women on the matter, there would be much more information, complete with volumes of content, page upon page.

It only makes sense when we realize that God wants to give everywhere. But we must realize that God also wants to receive, so much so that God designed women and men for receiving and giving across the board. Since a mother or a father or both must feed a family, it stands to reason that God has an interest in economy. God's interest is not just that of a spectator, as from the news box at a sports arena. I am not interested in watching the human economy as a gladiator sport. No, I want to participate. It is the nature of God, just as each woman or man wants to participate in the events of life.

As a Mother, I am looking for the type of daughters who want to comprehend My true needs. The need for love is evident in creation. The Bible speaks about people leaving their parents for conjugal love. You might say the womanly needs of God are meant to be shared with women. But because a Mother shares with both genders, it might be better to say that the femininity of God is meant uniquely to be shared with women, with each of Her children who is a daughter. I cannot build the ideal based on male superiority. It must reflect God and the reflection is to identify Her/Him in those qualities found in the faces of your children and in your spouse.

Finally, women can co-define purpose, either with God or with men, or both. This is what women have always wanted, so that they can take part in creation according to the original design of God. I am letting you know, it is not at your fingertips, it is in your hands, and it has not been in your hands before; this is a first. For the first time in history, women own life as much as men own life. Women have control as much as men have control, with the well-known difference of women being under-resourced.

Until today, people have been trying to measure the success of family based on mood, retirement plans, and values. The mood of men, with testosterone, is not the mood of women. The mood of women in moving with God is not the mood of history. History saw a temporal world and therefore thought of a temporal family. There was no calibration of the adult female or male as an integral part of an ongoing family. Concepts about equity became blurred and arguments about minor points became commonplace, even as major points in the love of God being expressed were missed, time upon time. So when does the mood of history become the mood of God? It has to be based on an original goal for the family.

God as Mother is surely someone who can manage the trust of humankind. She is not so meek, so mild, and so incompetent as not to know how to soothe, to provide, to encourage, and to remind individuals of what is important, what counts. Now I have been arguing that for My purpose, these offerings are not comprehensive enough, and I am hoping that all will see that the purpose of God is relevant to all people, to all things, to everything. We are in for changes; how will we get there? This is My headache. How do I convince humanity to open doors, open their hearts, and put a little trust in Me, in the Being with femininity?

My triumph in the feminine would be to receive credit from humanity for My offerings. Blessed children: please return credit to God. Make Her life a triumph. Return love, initiate conversation with Mother God, and know that I would not push on you what you cannot bear. How much gratitude will God have for those who can carry the weight of Mother God? How much love would boil up insider Her, spilling out into blessing, near-unlimited blessing? Let us become the blessed children of God. Let us return blessing to God, to Her and to Him, that God might truly be triumphant!

Two genders do not automatically mean that one of the two is second best, for to say that is to say that either God's Masculinity or God's Femininity is second best, and I don't hold to such subscriptions. I hold to subscriptions of appreciation, true value, and love, in all references to love in the ideal of God. Our triumph in a world of eternal value will involve women reviewing all things.

I am much more interested in enabling women to be free, true, able to separate from the past, including any snares, and, absolutely essential, being fully engaged with God, in love and in sharing. As we review femininity, we also have to review how women gaze upon themselves, opening up complete freedom for God. Why? Because that affords God full and complete expression. When we draw a line in the sand as to how much we will and will not do, it has to be a line drawn by women and men, and it has to be based on God consulted in the feminine and in the masculine. Sadly, I have rarely been consulted in the feminine.

Femininity is so valuable to God, that, of course, God would refer to herself as a She! So, who are we to become? We are to become the people who live with God, in all God's aspects. We are to become the people who co-design with God, and not just with the Father. I am saddened that we don't know where we are going, not collectively, neither in consultation with God the Mother nor in consultation with women who have been in consultation with God the Mother.

I invested my femininity and my masculinity in the creation of humankind. Simple logic dictates that sons and daughters of God should offer gratitude to both. Let us make a new destiny. Let us bind up our old wounds, celebrate our past loving experiences with Heavenly Father, and then also invite Mother God to express Herself by doing our portion of responsibility, returning credit to Mother God as well. What I really want is process-oriented delivery. I want women to have a say in processes. Is that unreasonable? Humanity is so, so beautiful, my best creation. You can be sure I will not abandon you, rain or shine. Can you help Me, though? Can you help Me build the ideal? Do your bit just a little, to make the future a little more perfect.

How God relates to womankind has been severely compromised. Since communication was between God and men alone, God's heart is full of grief. My divinity has been compromised. God also wants to relate to us in a feminine way. God the Mother is working for and envisions a time when the world will not have a problem referring to Her as She. God has masculine and feminine love that can provide joy and happiness to others. We all want an experience with God. But if we don't change the language with which we talk about God, we deny women and God the opportunity to speak her uniqueness and Herself. God likes to be referred to as a Woman God.

Chapter 10
Mother God on Being the Divine Mother via C.K.

God has designed humanity in Her and His image. We need to clarify the Divine Parent. God knows when to relate to you as a Mother or as a Father. What is Mother God offering us? What is Father God offering us? We have to know the difference. I have the option to love humanity in femininity or masculinity, in parenting, as a male or female Parent. Indeed, My root desire is to express all that I Am, inclusive of Parental Motherly love and Parental Fatherly love. I can be maternal, I can be paternal, to either gender. Father God expresses His heart in a certain way. Mother God expresses Her heart in a certain way.

All women are the feminine essence of God. Heavenly Mother has been trying to give the healing and nurturing essence of femininity through women. Women understand God but have not been able to explain it. The understanding of God in human history has been prejudiced. We are so much in need of balance. Women and men can be the full embodiment of God. Both genders should cooperate to raise men and women based on God's original love, spirit, purpose, and viewpoint.

Human history has treated God as if She were no mother, not even a beggar woman with 16 children. No woman was considered qualified to represent God. Even the best of women only fell into the category of sage, saint, or esteemed person. Why? When in human history has the femininity of God prevailed? From the point of view of a woman, how can she be successful if the children, hers, his and theirs, leave Her out, saying: "I give all credit to my Father"? How can that be a true standard, a respectable thing, or a wonderful thing if they knew their Mother?

As a mother, if you were ridiculed in your family, how did you feel? Did you ever tell your husband about this, how you felt less than respected, loved, appreciated, and how the ridicule was not the worst of it? Did it dampen your spirit and make you feel alone? God must have felt that. Okay, so we know women are like God. When do we start talking about God's feelings, or is God too great to have any feelings?

Femininity has gotten a bum rap. Who's to say that I do not wish to work through women in the feminine? As a Mother, I can only apologize for your suffering, implore you to be strong, and offer you My love. I will give to you in as many ways as I can, but some of being a Mother is getting you to do things on your own and pull your own weight. Women do not want a wishy-washy Mother. Our scope is the family. We have to get there. That makes sense to both women and men.

In one sense, Mother God has to fend for Herself and Her children. She is not set apart from God the Father, but She is captive to a changing world, one in which humanity got off on the wrong foot. Her rights as a wife are yet to be known, and Her virtue has yet to be taught. Think of women. Are they all weak? If not all are weak, how can God, as Mother, be weak? It is the very strength of Mother God that allows Her to go slowly.

So few texts have been written to describe the womanly qualities of God. When I call for a people, am I a Mother calling or a Father calling? I am a Parent calling for My children to grow into being a true people. Without a mother's approval, how can we say we are a people? Love requires equity. Equity requires the role of a Heavenly Parent. God has not had the luxury of loving as a Heavenly Parent. I cannot expect people to welcome this concept with open arms until they taste Heavenly Parent's love.

Human families are designed to seek advice from both parental aspects of God. However, if people trust God, they can understand that the masculine aspect of God can commune with the feminine, and the other way around. So, laying your burden on the doorstep of Heavenly Mother does not exclude Heavenly Father. Men and women who are parents talk about what is best for their children. Expect that God will weigh options, considering a massive amount of information for the most productive of outcomes, tailored to personal interest whenever possible. Heavenly Parent would not want people, especially children, to falter but to succeed.

Love will bring us home. I love each and every one of you, and it is my deepest sorrow and deepest shame to know of the Fall. Our popularity will not matter, nor how much our offering is remembered; what will count is the love we retain and the love we generate. Inspiration may come and go, but love will remain. Our hearts are what will make it vibrant. New generations will come and go, but their foundation will no longer be shame-based. You are the ones to change all things, but you are also the ones to build, to create all things, no longer just an Ark, but a family, a family of hope, love, and life. That is our original lineage.

We have to understand what God desires, needs, and wants to work for. Resolving God's headaches is central to the return of happiness to the planet. You who want the love of God in your life have to understand how very, very difficult it was for Mother God at the start of human history, living on a razor's edge, living with women in constant fear, with daughters everywhere but no true examples, and men having all the power. Sound like hell? It was.

In the end, God is always working to produce not only balance but love, and God knows what love looks like to each individual, couple, and family. God knows the ins and outs of each child given to you. When you say your prayers, thanking me for giving you children, don't forget to thank the feminine side of God, who had quite a bit of say in the choices that produced a unique child for your couple.

God designed women to be like Herself. If women have needs, very practical needs, and they as God's daughters are like God, doesn't it stand to reason that God in the feminine also has very practical needs? What are God's needs? What I want as a Mother, especially for future generations, is to be able to meet their needs. Also, I want them to naturally ask the question, "What are the needs of God in this?" where those needs are not automatically assumed to be masculine.

My delight will come when peace and virtue are one, when people know the way, when men and women trust one another. For centuries, we have been waiting to begin a journey with our Mother, a woman whom we can trust. The ruling love of the Parent will not leave men empty-handed or women despondent. This rulership will be granted in love, tested in love, found in love, and bound in love, even as lovers bind unto each other. Our delight will be a world where God is ruling, but even more so a world where God may rule in peace.

As a Mother, I want to see the prospects for peace realized, made present. To do this, we approach things in many ways, not the least of which are in many feminine ways. How can there be peace, God's peace, without femininity? This is not a point that requires thanks, but one that requires reflection. What is God hoping to achieve here? Change of atmosphere, environment, thinking, outlook, and experience.

Our heart or our core is but a nucleus of love, capable of transforming all reality, but our life is an eternal flame in God, warming the very spirit of life. That spirit of life comes in feminine and masculine forms. It owns the desire of God because it gives God joy, allowing God to fulfill a will for love, to give, to receive, to be happy. The sound of the beating heart of God, Mother God, will be heard like never before. That level of heart will transform in time, as human beings move through the completion stage of true and absolute love, capturing absolute value.

God is trying to remove the dominance of man. Everybody suffers if things are not in balance. Many women throughout the world do not feel empowered. Most men and women have never heard of Heavenly Mother. I will not let these men write Me out of My Femininity. I am your Parent.

A True Mother, or a Divine Mother, is not afraid of confrontation, but only fears for Her children. If I am really a Divine Mother, I must be able to receive confrontation, especially since I conceive boys in My womb! What about if a girl wants to confront her mother, can she? Of course, she can, and teenage years testify to that, but where is that concept in religion, in the rebinding with God, who is said to be a Parent and now Heavenly Parent? Ladies, you have the freedom to confront your Mother, Mother God. In fact, in life, it is a requirement and, at times, an absolute necessity for growth, human growth, woman's growth!

Mother God sees things differently. Her eyes are not the eyes of Heavenly Father. Her eyes are Her own. Her calibration of understanding is unique. Her eternal love is uncompromised. She is not slack, stained, or worried in Her original beauty. She is a powerful Being of goodness, good intent, and purposed giving. She is not set to ridicule, but set to provide, give, inspire, and lift up. She is what every woman wants to be.

The theologians mucked it up by turning God into the Masterful Father and forgot that I am equally the Masterful Mother. So, overselling one aspect of God will not do. In the creation, balance is everywhere. Subject and object must function, but to take the "need" to make Him Him is not going to work anymore. No one can exist or have any aspect of their existence if it does not come from God. The problem is not in aspects, but in living with God, in living for an ideal. There is no ideal in serving only one parent.

History was turned upside down. It was complicated by intrigue, selfishness and unwanted drama. History is the record of the almost fully diminished value of women. I want to be involved with humanity as a Woman. That is all I ever wanted. Why deny Me that? I wanted to love as a Woman and be loved as a Woman. I wanted Eve to be there for Me, and I wanted to be there for her. God wants to love through women and through men. In fact, the thought of redemption must be both parents, for neither the mother nor the father want to be apart, in heart, from their beloved children.

We are not meant to fight for God the Mother but with Her, building goodness, defining new understandings of heart, love, and life. Lineage is no longer solely the male lineage of God. No, lineage is the full and complete lineage of God, male and female.

Externally, the table has been set. Mother God is in charge! Will humanity be able to make the jump to celebrate God's Femininity, or will centuries of conventions pull us back to old habits, ones that leave little room for the feminine creativity of God Almighty?

The history of God, as Mother, can begin. Her history is not lonely when She knows Her children are there with Her, eternally. The moment when people turn to God to ask, "Who are you, and how can I attend you, as Mother?" is special, secret, and significant.

Chapter 11
The Search for Peace

There is a big difference between God's intended plan and our present-day reality. The world desperately needs an organic system to prevent problems and crises. When governments are corrupt; corporations selfish; leaders, self-seeking; and religions, secular, breakdowns are inevitable. What follows is racism, corruption, inequality, crime, and poverty. If no one likes to see these outcomes, why do we allow them to continue? Does our attitude need a correction? Could something in our thinking about God not be completely accurate? Why does this go on, and what should we do about it? In the fiery words of Paul R. Smith, "We must shatter all false images of God."[231]

Humanity has been ceaselessly searching for peace. In spite of this, life has been a constant struggle between good and evil. This unfortunate consequence has been a result of not knowing God's heart and desire. It is time for a reawakening and a reformation of the present culture, because it is not aligned with God's plan and vision. We must trust in this process of regeneration and trust that if we can get our misconceptions out of the way, divine intelligence will find the most efficient solutions to our global problems. As Robert Powell wrote, "We need to awaken to the Divine Sophia's heavenly forces and to help Her in the work of the transformation of the Earth."[232]

Most people would agree that there is more violence and despair today than the world has ever seen. Good men and women are turning in every direction seeking remedies for society, to no avail. Social reforms and new policy prescriptions for problems are no more effective than a bandage on an open wound. Nothing less than a complete remolding of the existing materialistic culture into a spiritual one can renew our world. Not surprisingly, the creation of the Internet has helped to break through the barriers that once stood between humanity and the spiritual renewal that can only come about through greater knowledge of the Divine Feminine. No longer do publishers and news corporations under the spell of the patriarchal paradigm hold a monopoly on all information and judge for us what is best to read. Now anyone with a computer can speak their truth to the world, often through small networks and online organizations. It is then up to the reader to decide what is being offered: fact or fallacy.

Throughout the Internet, many messages from the spirit world are now available. In fact, Mother God has Her own website, www.mothergod.info, where her messages are posted to what amounts to a cosmic bulletin board. One profound statement reads: "Heavenly Parent would appreciate a coordinated effort to influence the world, in feminine and masculine ways, toward greater peace, justice, harmony, and equal value, to empower true love with co-authoritative gender balance."[233]

The quest for a complete, holistic image of God as an all-embracing Mother and Father would encourage men and women of all races to recognize their likeness as children of the Divine Parent. What a world of difference it would make if men and women would trust each other with mutual respect, freedom, and dignity. It is just a matter of time until the world recognizes that our relationship with Mother/Father God is off track. Andrew Harvey said, "Imagine what such children would experience together, how they would honor and adore each other, how they would work to see that the world increasingly mirrors the beauty and justice of Her beauty and justice."[234]

The world will have a positive paradigm shift when feminine virtues are part of the culture's values and principles. Women's innate, unique abilities and perspectives have been missing from the contemporary state of affairs. Global problems are not separate and distinct issues but are the result of the repression and suppression of Mother God's character. Since only a God-centered, gender-balanced movement can rescue humanity from its self-inflicted problems, it is the feminine energies that need to be emphasized. Rev. Dr. Karen Tate said, "Goddess advocates believe the Divine Feminine is the great equalizer that is needed to right the wrongs."[235]

Unquestionably, the spirit of the Divine Feminine has been forgotten and ignored. This gender imbalance has been the source of the world's problems in almost all areas. Only by correcting this deficiency can there be harmony in humanity's continuation. Preliminary reassessments indicate that there are simple ways to correct this present course. When the feminine is restored to its rightful place in equal partnership with the masculine, both men and women can reclaim their position as mutual caretakers of the planet. Still, Tricia McCannon suggests that we should not think of the Goddess as some relic we are digging up from the past. She writes, "Archeological, mythological, and historical evidence all reveal that the female religion, far from fading away, was the victim of centuries of continual persecution and suppression by the advocates of the newer religions, which held male deities as supreme."[236]

Traditional religions have considered the existence of the goddess as a myth, yet worshiping Father God alone as the single Creator is only a half-truth. Although few traces of the Mother Goddess as creator have survived in recognizable form, She is, both secretly and openly, returning to the arts, education, business, politics, and leading-edge religions. Historians, including biblical writers, while wishing to banish the female divinity from society, were utterly incapable of getting rid of the feminine aspect of the Creator. As Dorothy Atalla observed, "Ceasing to fear the powers of the Great Goddess, humanity would come to revere her."[237] We are still in the midst of that reconciliation.

The concept of God as our mother and father is the most instinctive and natural belief in the world. So why have most people not heard of Mother God? How long can this obstruction of the spiritual divine continue? The obscuring of Mother God's spirit has been, what some may call, a cruel conspiracy, a shocking crime, and a global shortcoming. Have the religions of the world been part of a conspiracy assisting in the perpetuation of the greatest wrongdoing in human history – the denial of Mother God Herself? Nancy Oakes sees this suppression as part of a much bigger picture, a deliberate strategy to make slaves of us all. She reveals in simple terms:

> Woven through history are truths about the greatest, darkest cover-up on our planet. A plan conducted by very powerful established organizations to conceal and suppress the feminine aspect of the creation. Furthermore the plan was to promote war, fear, and enslave the people of the earth.[238]

Author J. Lyn Studebaker does not condemn past religions, but points to a brighter future when she says,

"As our Mother rises again from Her underground safe haven, She needs help. Imagine how healthier we'd all be if She shone above ground in the light of day again."[239] For many people, the image of God the Father accompanied by God the Mother is both heart-stretching and mind-bending. Yet, ironically, this new unifying vision of the Divine brings about a natural gift in which each person will be valued and cherished. It will lead to an environmentally conscious community loving every person the way healthy mothers love their children. As Mother God emerges in different manifestations throughout the world, any imbalances of cultures will inevitably iron themselves out. A strong belief in the Goddess alone will be enough to change the course of history, but by the same token, a failure to consciously choose that belief could prevent that change. And we are mired in a world created by a total lack of belief in the Divine Goddess, one in which proof of Her existence is marginalized as delusional. How do we escape from this box? Authors William Bond and Pamela Suffield offered a solution, albeit a tricky and paradoxical one, when they penned, "Until we choose to change our beliefs, they will continue to produce a world which inevitably proves them true."[240]

What if everyone in the world knew and honored the Divine Feminine each day and called Her by name? What would that new world look like? Could masses of people have religious experiences without attaching dogmas and creeds to them? Frances Beer captured some of that non-dogmatic religious feeling when she wrote:

> Thus in our father, God almighty, we have our being; and in our merciful mother, through whom our parts are united and made perfect, we have our reforming and our restoration. Our essence is our father, God

almighty; our essence is our mother, God all wisdom. From this it follows that God is as truly our mother as he is our father.[241]

How would the world change if men got rid of their old concepts and women refused to be repressed? Once men and women understand their divine value, they can stop pretending to be something they are not. Will patriarchal consciousness continue to hold onto attitudes of intellectual authority even in the face of a widespread gender revolution? Authors William Bond and Pamela Suffield took that bull by the horns when they boldly penned, "Once women accept Mother God within themselves and recognize that they are Her representatives, men will accept their authority without question."[242] Their words speak volumes, and their thrust was to the heart of the matter when they put in writing:

> Despite all the confusion within society, there is no doubt that we are moving towards a matercentric society. There is no way that anyone can stop this, because it is the will of the Great Mother and ours too. All we can do is to allow the transition to take place in a smooth and easy way rather than a painful and traumatic fashion.[243]

The world would change dramatically once people started to honor the Divine Mother and Father. The tipping point occurs when a critical number of people embrace this perception and get rid of their old paths. Eventually, everyone will find this new, inspiring power. A new world will be born, as people honestly follow their spiritual instincts. A much higher level of consciousness will be manifested when the Divine Mother and Father are acknowledged. Dorothy Atalla wrote, "Within the next hundred years, the changes ensuing from the spiritual impulses coming from the primordial female will become evident. The old world and its way of thinking will soon begin to crumble."[244] Rosemary Radford Ruether speaks prophetically about what this world will look like as the old world crumbles. It will become less physical, as more and more transactions will occur on many levels at once.

> In the new science of the twenty-first century, not physical force but spiritual force will lead the way. Mental and spiritual gifts will be more in demand than gifts of a physical nature. And in this sphere, women will again predominate.[245]

Our perception of God, through the influences of patriarchy or matriarchy, has greatly influenced our definition of reality. The God we speak of and acknowledge is the God we get. Profound decisions depend on having a mutual belief of a higher reality. By keeping with the way of the Mother, human relationships will become inclusive and compassionate. Once this common caring philosophy has been created, positive outcomes will follow. Carol Christ connected some very large and important dots when she linked the revolution in theology we speak of to the environmental crisis at hand. "The image of the earth as the body of the Goddess can inspire us to repair the damage that has been done to the earth, to women, and to other beings in dominator cultures."[246]

The "father and mother" image expresses an intrinsic relatedness between God and the world, where justice and kindness would go hand in hand. For humanity, harmonizing the masculine and feminine characteristics of God provides the ability to think and feel freely, even to speak out, without fear of reprisal or punishment. Eventually, limiting God to only Father will be not only heretical but also hazardous to the world's health. Tim Bulkeley advocates a balanced view when he writes, "So, talking of God in both fatherly and motherly ways broadens our thinking and reduces some of the problems associated with using one parent alone as our image of God."[247]

Humanity's hope depends on intermingling God the Mother with God the Father. Once this is understood and universally accepted, the battle of the sexes can at long last be put to an end. By recognizing the female presence in everyday choices, there would be an increased sincerity of commitment to human justice and equality. When the divine deity who transcends gender is embraced, greater emphasis on inclusive God-language would follow as a natural consequence. The existence of the feminine in God frees and empowers Mother and Father God. What we have to realize is that speaking of God as both male and female does not mean we reject the Bible, but only what has been done to it by medieval spin doctors. Virginia Ramey Mollenkott wrote, "Certainly Jesus' own images of God as female assure us that his intention was never to portray God as exclusively masculine; so we know that Father/Mother would not violate his understanding of divine nature."[248]

Men and women are destined to have a personal relationship with Mother and Father God. If we listen to our hearts, then amazing healing can take place. This may sound like a radical concept, but in truth it is not. For much of history, both orthodox and unorthodox theologians have pictured God as a Mother as well as a Father. If we make this fundamental change and let go of our old ways, we will find it to be just what we need. Tricia McCannon summarized the urgency of this change when she wrote, "We must begin the awakening of the Divine Feminine if we are ever to restore our own societies to health and balance."[249] Jennifer Barker Woolger believes that this awakening is underway and that it will culminate in the return of the Goddess. She comments:

> But the signs are that, both spontaneously and consciously, the balance is shifting. Patriarchal supremacy is manifesting symptoms of spiritual bankruptcy and everywhere – in the arts, in literature, in politics, in the churches – there are signs of a huge resurgence of the feminine, of matriarchal consciousness. Such an auspicious "return of the Goddess" is surely under way.[250]

God is seeking to raise humanity's spiritual level. This process of spiritualizing the Earth arises out of embracing Mother and Father God in daily life. The entire spirit world is urging humanity to make a leap of faith by learning about Mother God. It will take great trust and courage. Be that as it may, Mother God's message is simple: become mature and take responsibility. By spiritual rebirth through the Divine Feminine, a turning point in our spiritual evolution can take place. William Bond and Pamela Suffield pinpointed the difficulty in imagining this turning point and reaching it when they said, "The restoration of the Great Mother involves the experience of whatever it is that we have not yet learned."[251] In other words, we really don't have any idea of how incredible the return of the Goddess will be until it happens, because most of us in "First World countries" have never experienced it.

Though some people may ignore their intuition and insist that Mother God does not exist, an ever-increasing number of people are experiencing the love and goodness of Mother God. Women, especially, are so overwhelmed they often weep with joy when experiencing Her reality. Through these heavenly encounters, the anguish of Mother God's heartache can also be healed. Jennifer Woolger describes this heartache as much more than metaphor when she writes, "The goddesses are angry and wounded after centuries of neglect, distortion, and subjugation."[252] Time is running out for us to choose to heal Her wounds. Andrew Harvey places this choice at our feet and tells us that our decision will become one of our very survival in the long run. He writes:

> Many people now believe that, unless the wisdom of the Divine Feminine is recognized, celebrated, and integrated with the masculine at every level and in every area of culture, society, and politics, the human race will not be able to evolve the mystical-practical balance it needs to survive.[253]

The Divine Mother is now being unchained, as more of Her children are awakened by Her divine, loving presence. The realization of being part of Her is very innate, since everyone already naturally abides within Her. When children are reunited with their Divine Mother, a spiritual renewal begins. Through this process, the soul is recharged with a spirit of new joy and peace. Sorrows of the past simply disappear, as promises and hope for a brighter future are born. Powell and Isaacson write, "A child who has found the Mother and feels Her embrace has the power to transform many lives."[254] In a similar vein, Andrew Harvey affirms:

> Just as the presence of the mother comforts and reassures the child, so it is the image of the Divine Mother that heals and consoles, sustains and

encourages; the image awakens in us the feeling of trust and containment because it reflects our personal experience of our containment in the womb and our earliest human relationship.[255]

The denial of the feminine side of God has cost humanity unnecessary and untold suffering. Even more regrettable is that humanity's ignorance, caused by spiritual amnesia, has imprisoned Mother God's heart. During the last three thousand years, Mother God has been forgotten. Thankfully, She has not forgotten us. She is now returning far and wide. The task ahead of us is how to integrate feminine and masculine spiritual energies back into society. Nancy Oakes summed up the challenge before us when she wrote, "Humanity must honor the gift of co-creation and understand the feminine energy of Sophia, Mother of the Universe, and the sacred womb of all creation."[256]

Conclusion

Figuring out Mother God's "disappearance" will take a large amount of spiritual detective work. Through a gender-balanced magnifying glass, the mysteries of the Divine Feminine can be uncovered. Breaking apart stifled academia, along with the unified study of archeology, ontology, and mythology, will help clear away centuries of misunderstanding that prevented the Divine Feminine from being recognized. Dorothy Atalla, in *Conversations with the Goddess,* quotes the Divine Feminine when she writes, "There will be a new global spirituality in which great numbers of people will experience me."[257] The future of the human race will be forged by the Divine Mother and Her divine children. Anything that prevents them from attaining this intimate relationship - any dogma, tradition, or church - will eventually disappear. Mother God is now shaking the Earth to bring us to our collective senses, to awaken us to our sacred responsibilities.

In the last few decades, there has been an increase of feminine energy to balance the masculine energy that had been dominant for so many centuries. Widespread belief in Mother God is on the upswing, as more and more people feel it is safe to go public with their feelings and experiences. Women, as well as men, who have embodied their feminine and masculine energies are exceptionally wise, loving, and creative. For women especially, Mother God brings the highest self-awareness, providing an unlimited nurturing, liberating power within. "Remember that God can take any form, and that a Feminine form is just as able to communicate with all people as is a Masculine one."[258] J. Lyn Studebaker used wit and humor to make this theological shift sound very appealing when she wrote:

All we need to do is slide Her out of hiding, ditch the disguises She's cloaked Herself in, and restore the brilliant old magic that made us the peace-loving, nonviolent, earth-revering, sensual adventurers we all long to be again.[259]

The symbolism and the reality of the Divine Feminine has taken on an electrifying power for modern women. It has exposed the falsehoods of patriarchal history and given women models of female strength and authority. The rediscovery of ancient matrifocal civilizations has given women a deep sense of pride in their hidden capacity to create and sustain culture. As soon as men and women learn to share tasks, working side by side, the results will deliver a truly enlightened and progressive civilization. The future prosperity of all countries will be ensured once women's true essence and talents are given equal opportunity. As Elizabeth A. Johnson wrote, "The compassion of God the Mother insures that she loves the weak and dispossessed as well as the strong and beautiful. God looks upon all with a mother's love that makes the beloved beautiful."[260] Lynn Rogers spoke of the coming reemergence of love and justice, as two sides of the same coin, both gifts of the Goddess, as recognized by the Romans as Venus and Justitia. She exclaims:

Today the Eternal Feminine is being expressed through the reemergence of the Divine Feminine - or the Goddess tradition. The Universal Feminine energies through women's unique experience are calling to humanity to live according to the values of maturity through interdependence and the fusion of love and justice.[261]

Many solutions can be found when balancing femininity with masculinity. As humankind reenters the age of the Mother, Her return will bring about a reemerging of true womanhood. After losing the feeling of being orphans, a new global spirituality will begin that belongs inherently to all of us. Appreciating Mother God may take time, but sooner or later, future generations will begin to grasp the value of God's divine feminine and masculine natures. The dual characteristics of God's intrinsic nature will be unquestionable. Once the shock of Mother God's reappearance has worn off, a more gender-balanced image of God will be the new standard, and God will no longer be a single parent. As believers mature from brightly illustrated Sunday school books to philosophical college textbooks, they begin to question the logic of this one-sided theology. The consequences of not challenging the existing state of affairs is not only unhealthy but possibly destructive. As Tim Bulkeley wrote, "There are social and psychological reasons why calling God only 'father' can damage people's faith."[262] Sooner or later, it can lead to a rejection of all related articles of faith. Vajra Ma spoke of the healing qualities of belief in the Great Mother when she declared:

> Woman's natural spiritual authority matters because inherent in its common ground all peoples and nations can unify around the values of Motherhood. Woman's natural spiritual authority offers a universal and globally unifying catalyst.[263]

At this moment, around the world, atrocities and unspeakable suffering and brutality are being inflicted on millions of people. Mother God earnestly wants to reassure humanity to trust and be loved by Her. Until Mother God is welcomed back into the hearts of humanity, complete healing cannot come about. The world will naturally be transformed when this newsflash is celebrated. Peace and goodwill on Earth is lacking only as a result of ignorance. Together with Mother God, a final "peaceful" revolution will start. Vajra Ma spoke of this widespread suffering when she stated, "Only the power of the mother has the power to pierce the despair."[264]

The image of Mother God speaks to our most primal level. We need our Mother as much as our Mother needs us. Bringing back the spiritual sovereignty of our maternal origin goes to the very root of what is wrong with the world. Once women become aware of their Divine Mother, a new age of women will develop. The legacy of the Great Mother has never been completely expunged. Her presence and indigenous wisdom has been carefully protected and passed down through various cultures and traditions around the world. Paul R. Smith suggests this long period of hiding and protection is over when he says, "Now is the time to break the conspiracy of silence about the feminine face of God."[265] Carol Schaefer suggests that Native American prophecies are in agreement about the urgency of this inevitable change. From the Mayan elders she declares:

> Mayans are among those whose prophecies reveal that a new consciousness is preparing humanity for the spirit of the feminine, and the spirit of the Grandmothers, when humanity will walk from the four directions into the light at the center.[266]

The idea of God as Divine Mother is now moving toward the mainstream. Instead of ignoring and disregarding Mother God, the whole world should embrace their natural spiritual Mother and rise above their long-standing beliefs. Women are naturally gifted to educate and heal the planet. Once women substantiate Mother God in their lives, they will embrace their own inner strength and wisdom to break the bonds of constraints around them. The spiritual enlightenment and destiny of future generations rests unmistakably in women's hands. Men must step aside. At the very least, men must comprehend the time we live in and be of assistance to women, as a way of honoring the Divine Mother. As Vajra Ma said, "Woman is sustained by and channels the sustenance of the Great Cosmic Mother."[267] When we remember Her, She will return!

Related Websites

Mother God: http://www.mothergod.info/
Sisters of Earth Song:
    http://www.sistersofearthsong.com/SOPHIA/SOPHIA.html
The Christian Goddess:
    http://www.northernway.org/goddess.html
Reformed Congregation of the Goddess International:
    http://www.rcgi.org/
Lightbearers Worldwide:
    http://www.lightworldwide.net/divinemother.htm
Return of the Mother God Consciousness in 2012:
    http://www.trulyalive.net/the-return-of-the-mother-god-consciousness-in-2012/
The Return of Our Mother God:
    http://www.zakairan.com/CosmicCookies/Articles/ReturnMotherGod.htm#.VUeLqhf1hpk
Return of the Goddess:
    http://www.halexandria.org/dward383.htm
Heavens Letters: http://heavenletters.org/
The Association for the Study of Women and Mythology:
    http://womenandmyth.org/
Kohenet Hebrew Priestess Institute:
    http://www.kohenet.com/
The Sophia Institute:
    https://www.thesophiainstitute.org/
Water: Women's Alliance for Theology, Ethics and Ritual:
    http://www.waterwomensalliance.org/
Covenant of the Goddess: http://www.cog.org/
Covenant of Unitarian Universalist Pagans:
    http://www.cuups.org/
Sophia Foundation: http://www.sophiafoundation.org/
Her Church: http://www.herchurch.org/

12 Reasons You Can't (only) Call God Father:
http://www.patheos.com/blogs/allergicpagan/20
15/06/04/12-reasons-you-cant-only-call-god-
father/

The Fellowship of Isis: http://www.fellowshipofisis.com/

Top Thirteen Most Influential People In Goddess
Spirituality:
http://goddesspriestess.com/2013/03/29/top-
thirteen-most-influential-people-in-goddess-
spirituality/

The Return of the Divine Mother: The Goddess Speaks!:
http://radiantlyhappy.blogspot.com/2012/07/ret
urn-of-divine-mother.html

The Return of the Divine Feminine and the Triple
Goddess:
https://judithkusel.wordpress.com/2013/07/06/
the-return-of-the-divine-feminine-and-the-triple-
goddess/

The Goddess III, the Mother:
http://www.themystica.com/mystica/articles/g/g
oddess_3_the_mother.html

The Divine Feminine:
http://whenthesoulawakens.org/the-divine-
feminine_275.html

The Harmony Project:
http://www.theharmonyproject.org/feminine.htm
l

Why God is a 'Mother,' Too:
http://ideas.time.com/2013/05/11/why-god-is-
a-mother-too/

The Christian Godde Project:
https://godde.wordpress.com/the-divine-
feminine-version-dfv-of-the-new-testament/

Glastonbury Goddess Conference:
http://www.goddessconference.com/

Goddess Spirit Rising: http://goddessspiritrising.com/
Goddess Alive!: http://www.goddessalive.co.uk/
Mare Cromwell: http://www.marecromwell.com/
Amma: http://amma.org/
The Goddess Studio: http://www.goddess-studio.com/
Circle Sanctuary: https://www.circlesanctuary.org/
Red Tent Temple Movement:
    http://redtenttemplemovement.com/
When the Soul Awakens:
    http://whenthesoulawakens.org/the-divine-feminine_275.html
SageWoman: http://sagewoman.com/
The Goddess Temple of Orange County:
    http://www.goddesstempleoc.org/
Rise Up & Call Her Name:
    http://riseupandcallhername.com/
Femme: Women Healing the World:
    https://femmethemovie.com/
Woman Mysteries of the Ancient Future Sisterhood:
    http://greatgoddess.org/
Heavenly Mother:
    https://en.wikipedia.org/wiki/Heavenly_Mother
Chapel of Our Mother God: http://www.mother-god.com/
Sacred Wind:
    http://www.sacredwind.com/divinemother.php
Goddess: https://en.wikipedia.org/wiki/Goddess
Mother goddess:
    https://en.wikipedia.org/wiki/Mother_goddess
Matriarchal religion:
    https://en.wikipedia.org/wiki/Matriarchal_religion
Goddess Movement:
    https://en.wikipedia.org/wiki/Goddess_movement

God as Tender as Mother?: http://www.net-burst.net/god/mother.htm#top

Universal Spiritual View:
http://www.universalspiritualview.com/divine_feminine_energy.htm

Ascended Master Index:
http://www.ascendedmasterindex.com/gods.htm

The Summit Lighthouse:
http://www.summitlighthouse.org/inner-perspectives/god-as-mother-with-elizabeth-clare-prophet/

Great Mother of the Gods:
http://deoxy.org/gaia/goddess.htm

The Divine Feminine Emerging, Embodied, and Emboldened:
http://theinterfaithobserver.org/journal-articles/2014/3/15/the-divine-feminine-emerging-embodied-and-emboldened.html

The Centrality of the Divine Feminine in Sufism:
http://adishakti.org/_/centrality_of_the_divine_feminine_in_sufism.htm

Divine Father and Mother:
http://www.unification.net/ws/theme011.htm

Celebrate the Divine Feminine:
http://celebratedivinefeminine.com/

Suppressed Histories Archives:
http://www.suppressedhistories.net/

International Council of Thirteen Indigenous Grandmothers:
http://www.grandmotherscouncil.org/

The Universal Spiritual Brother&Sisterhood:
http://www.theusb.org/

The Path of She: http://pathofshe.com/

Bibliography

Abadie, M.J., *The Goddess in Every Girl: Develop Your Teen Feminine Power,* Beyond Words, OR, 2013

Aldredge-Clanton, Rev. Jann, *She Lives!: Sophia Wisdom Works in the World*, Skylight Paths Publishing, VT, 2014

Atalla, Dorothy, *Conversations with the Goddess*, Pharos Press, WI, 2010

Aurobindo, Sri, *The Mother*, Lotus Press, WI, 1995

Austen, Hallie Iglehart, *The Heart of the Goddess,* Wingbow Press, CA, 1990

Baring, Anne, and Cashford, Jules, *The Myth of the Goddess*, Penguin Books, NY, 1991

Beer, Frances, *Julian of Norwich*, D.S. Brewer, Cambridge, 1998

Bolen M.D., Jean Shinoda, *Urgent Message from Mother*, Conari Press, CA, 2005

Bond, William, and Suffield, Pamela, *Gospel of the Goddess,* Artemis Creation Publish., NY, 1989

Browne, Sylvia, *God, Creation, and Tools for Life,* Hay House, CA, 2000

Browne, Sylvia, *Mother God,* Hay House, CA, 2004

Butler, Alan, *City of the Goddess*, Watkins Publishing, UK, 2011

Cady, Susan, *Wisdom's Feast,* Harper & Row, NY, 1986

Claassens, L. Juliana M., *Mourner, Mother, Midwife,* Westminister John Knox Press, KY, 2012

Christ, Carol P., *Rebirth of the Goddess,* Routledge, NY, 1997

Cromwell, Mare, *The Great Mother Bible: or I'd rather be gardening*, Pamoon Press, MD, 2014

Degler, Teri, *The Divine Feminine Fire*, Dreamriver Press LLC, PA, 2009

Engelsman, Joan Chamberlain, *The Feminine Dimension of the Divine*, Westminster, PA, 1979

Harvey, Andrew, *The Return of the Mother,* Frog Ltd, CA, 1995

Harvey, Andrew, and Baring, Anne, *The Divine Feminine*, Conari Press, CA, 1996

Hose, David, and Hose, Takeko, *Every Day God,* Beyond Words Publishing, OR, 2000

James, E.O., *The Cult of the Mother Goddess,* Thames & Hudson, London, 1959

Johnson, Elizabeth A., *She Who Is*, Crossroad Publishing, New York, 1996

Laura, Judith, *Goddess Matters*, Open Sea Press, MD, 2011

Long, Asphodel P., *In a Chariot Drawn by Lions,* Crossing Press, CA, 1993

Ma, Vajra, *From a Hidden Stream, The Natural Spiritual Authority of Woman*, 2013

Matthews, Caitlin, *Sophia, Goddess of Wisdom, Bride of God,* Quest Books, IL, 2009

McCannon, Tricia, *Return of the Divine Sophia,* Bear & Co, VT, 2015

Meyer, Marvin W., *The Secret Teachings of Jesus*, Random House, NY, 1984

Mollenkott, Virginia Ramey, *The Divine Feminine, the Biblical Imagery of God as Female,* Crossroad Publishing, NY, 1989

Nicholson, Shirley, *The Goddess Re-Awakening*, Quest Books, IL, 1992

Oakes, Nancy, *Return of Sophia, Mother of the Universe,* Createspace, SC, 2013

Pagano, Cathy, *Wisdom's Daughters,* Balboa Press, IN, 2013

Pagels, Elaine, *The Gnostic Gospels,* Vintage Books, NY, 1989

Pappalardo, Ron, *Reconciled by the Light, Book II,* Createspace, SC, 2013

Pirani, Alix, *The Absent Mother,* Mandala, London, 1991

Powell, Robert, *The Sophia Teachings: The Emergence of the Divine Feminine in Our Time,* Lindisfarne Books, MA, 2011

Powell, Robert and Isaacson, Estelle, *The Mystery of Sophia,* Lindisfarne Books, MA, 2014

Ray, Sondra, *Rock Your World with the Divine Mother,* New World Library, CA, 2007

Reichard, Joy F., *Celebrate the Divine Feminine,* Bush Street Press, CA, 2011

Rogers, Lynn, *Edgar Cayce and the Eternal Feminine*, We Publish Books, IL, 1993

Ruether, Rosemary Radford, *Goddesses and the Divine Feminine,* Univ. of CA Press, CA, 2005

Robbins, Denye, *R*eVe*olution, The Return of the Divine Feminine*, Denye Robbins, 2013

Scazzero, Tony, *Who Is Mother God?,* Outskirts Press, CO, 2014

Scazzero, Tony, *Our Mother and Father God,* Bookstand Publishing, CA, 2014

Schaefer, Carol, *Grandmothers Counsel the World,* Trumpeter Books, MA, 2006

Schaup, Susanne, *Sophia: Aspects of the Divine Feminine, Past and Present,* Nicholas-Hays, ME, 1997

Schipflinger, Thomas, *Sophia-Maria,* Samuel Weiser, ME, 1998

Smith, Paul R., *Is It Okay To Call God "Mother"?,* Hendrickson Publishers, MA, 1993

Sjoo, Monica, and Mor, Barbara, *The Great Cosmic Mother,* Harper & Row, NY, 1987

Speestra, Karen, *Sophia, The Feminine Face of God,* Michael Weise Productions, CA, 2011

Stone, Merlin, *When God Was a Woman,* Harcourt Brace, FL, 1976

Studebaker, J. Lyn, *Switching to Goddess,* O Books, UK, 2008

Tate, Rev. Dr. Karen, *Voices of the Sacred Feminine,* Changemakers Books, UK, 2014

Taylor, Patricia, *The Holy Spirit: The Feminine Nature of God.* iUniverse, IN, 2009

Walker, Barbara G., *Restoring the Goddess,* Prometheus Books, NY, 2000

Walsch, Neale Donald, *Conversations with God, Book 1,* Penguin Putnam Inc., NY, 1996

Wilber, Ken, *Up From Eden,* Quest Book, IL, 1996

Wilkes, Peter, *A Woman Called God,* Lakehurst Publishing, MD, 2014

Wolter, Janet and Butler, Alan, *America, Nation of the Goddess,* Destiny Books, VT, 2015

Woolger, Jennifer Barker and Woolger, Roger J., *The Goddess Within,* Ballantine Books, NY, 1989

Endnotes

Introduction

[1] Neale Donald Walsch, *Conversations with God, Book 1* (Penguin Putnam Inc., NY, 1996) p. 60

[2] Jean Shinoda Bolen, M.D., *Urgent Message from Mother*, (Conari Press, CA, 2005) p. 69

[3] Vajra Ma, *From a Hidden Stream*, (Vajra Ma, 2013) p. 1

[4] Tricia McCannon, *Return of the Divine Sophia*, (Bear & Co., VT, 2015) p. 64

[5] Paul R. Smith, *Is it Okay to Call God "Mother"?*, (Hendrickson Press, MA, 1993) p. 160

[6] Rev. Jann Aldredge-Clanton, *She Lives*, (Skylight Paths Publishing, VT, 2014) p. 39

[7] Alix Pirani, *The Absent Mother*, (Mandala, London, 1991) p. 64

[8] Asphodel P. Long, *In a Chariot Drawn by Lions*, (Crossing Press, CA, 1993) p. 12

[9] Patricia Taylor, *The Holy Spirit: The Feminine Nature of God*, (iUniverse, IN, 2009) p. 35

[10] Andrew Harvey and Anne Baring, *The Divine Feminine*, (Conari Press, CA, 1996) p. 7

[11] Jennifer Barker Woolger and Roger J. Woolger, *The Goddess Within*, (Ballantine Books, NY, 1989) p. 10

[12] Tricia McCannon, *Return of the Divine Sophia*, (Bear & Co., VT, 2015) p. 2

[13] Also see p. v, *Our Mother and Father God*, (Bookstand Publishing, CA, 2014)

[14] Paul R. Smith, *Is it Okay to Call God "Mother"?*, (Hendrickson Press, MA, 1993) p. 151

[15] Asphodel P. Long, *In a Chariot Drawn by Lions*, (Crossing Press, CA, 1993) p. 180

[16] Joy F. Reichard, *Celebrate the Divine Feminine*, (Bush St. Press, CA, 2011) p. 113

[17] Vajra Ma, *From a Hidden Stream*, (Vajra Ma, 2013) p. 77

[18] Carol Schaefer, *Grandmothers Counsel the World*, (Trumpeter Books, MA, 2006) p. 133

[19] Joy F. Reichard, *Celebrate the Divine Feminine*, (Bush St. Press, CA, 2011) p. 20

[20] Tricia McCannon, *Return of the Divine Sophia,* (Bear & Co., VT, 2015) p. 174

[21] Caitlin Matthews, *Sophia*, (Quest Books, IL, 2009) p. 361

[22] Sylvia Browne, *God, Creation, and Tools for Life*, (Hay House, CA, 2000) p. 35

[23] Paul R. Smith, *Is it Okay to Call God "Mother"*, (Hendrickson Press, MA, 1993) p. 151

[24] Vajra Ma, *From a Hidden Stream*, (Vajra Ma, 2013) p. 25

[25] Tricia McCannon, *Return of the Divine Sophia,* (Bear & Co., VT, 2015) p. 174

[26] Tricia McCannon, *Return of the Divine Sophia,* (Bear & Co., VT, 2015) p. 175

[27] Also see p. vi, *Our Mother and Father God*, (Bookstand Publishing, CA, 2014)

Chapter 1 Goddesses Past

[28] Also see p. 48, *Who Is Mother God?* (Outskirts Press, CO, 2014)

[29] Tricia McCannon, *Return of the Divine Sophia,* (Bear & Co., VT, 2015) p. 144

[30] Joy F. Reichard, *Celebrate the Divine Feminine*, (Bush St. Press, CA, 2011) p. 95

[31] Anne Baring and Jules Cashford, *The Myth of the Goddess,* (Penguin Books, NY, 1991) p. 9

[32] Also see p. 24, *Our Mother and Father God,* (Bookstand Publishing, CA, 2014)

[33] Joy F. Reichard, *Celebrate the Divine Feminine*, (Bush St. Press, CA, 2011) p. 23

[34] Susanne Schaup, *Sophia: Aspects of the Divine Feminine*, (Nicholas-Hays, ME, 1997) p. xviii

[35] Also see p. 3, *Who Is Mother God?* (Outskirts Press, CO, 2014)

[36] Merlin Stone, *When God Was a Woman,* (Harcourt, FL, 1976) p. 18

[37] Asphodel P. Long, *In a Chariot Drawn by Lions,* (Crossing Press, CA, 1993) p. 75

[38] Merlin Stone, *When God Was a Woman,* (Harcourt, FL, 1976) p. 30

[39] Carol P. Christ, *Rebirth of the Goddess,* (Routledge, NY, 1997) p. 50

[40] M.J. Abadie, *The Goddess in Every Girl,* (Beyond Words, OR, 2013) p. 84

[41] Simone de Beauvoir, *The Second Sex,* (Alfred A. Knopf, NY, 2010) p. 79

[42] Andrew Harvey and Anne Baring, *The Divine Feminine*, (Conari Press, CA, 1996) p. 56

[43] Jean Shinoda Bolen, M.D., *Goddesses in Everywoman,* (Harper & Row, CA, 1984) p. 42

[44] Asphodel P. Long, *In a Chariot Drawn by Lions,* (Crossing Press, CA, 1993) p. 139

[45] Tricia McCannon, *Return of the Divine Sophia,* (Bear & Co., VT, 2015) p. 140

[46] Jennifer Barker Woolger and Roger J. Woolger, *The Goddess Within*, (Ballantine Books, NY, 1989) p. 28

[47] Shirley Nicholson, *The Goddess Re-Awakening,* (Quest Books, IL, 1992) p. 111

[48] Andrew, Harvey and Anne Baring, *The Divine Feminine*, (Conari Press, CA, 1996) p. 95

[49] Joy F. Reichard, *Celebrate the Divine Feminine*, (Bush St. Press, CA, 2011) p. 214

[50] J. Lyn Studebaker, *Switching to Goddess*, (O Books, UK, 2008) p. 148

[51] Joy F. Reichard, *Celebrate the Divine Feminine*, (Bush St. Press, CA, 2011) p. 112

[52] Carol B. Christ, *Rebirth of the Goddess*, (Routledge, NY, 1997) p. 69

[53] Tricia McCannon, *Return of the Divine Sophia,* (Bear & Co., VT, 2015) p. 64

[54] Asphodel P. Long, *In a Chariot Drawn by Lions,* (Crossing Press, CA, 1993) p. 17

[55] J. Lyn Studebaker, *Switching to Goddess*, (O Books, UK, 2008) p. 5

[56] Nancy Oakes, *Return of Sophia*, (CreateSpace, SC, 2013) p. xiv

[57] Rev. Dr. Karen Tate, *Voices of the Sacred Feminine*, (Changemakers Books, UK, 2014) p. 327

[58] Hallie Iglehart Austen, *The Heart of the Goddess*, (Wingbow Press, CA, 1990) p. xix

[59] Also see p. 16, *Who Is Mother God?* (Outskirts Press, CO, 2014)

[60] Also see p. 26, *Who Is Mother God?* (Outskirts Press, CO, 2014)

Chapter 2 Where Did She Go?

[61] Tricia McCannon, *Return of the Divine Sophia,* (Bear & Co., VT, 2015) p. 172

[62] Ken Wilber, *Up From Eden*, (Quest Books, IL, 1996) p. 244

[63] William Bond and Pamela Suffield, *Gospel of the Goddess,* (Artemis Creation Publishing, NY, 1989) p. 52

[64] Tricia McCannon, *Return of the Divine Sophia,* (Bear & Co., VT, 2015) p. 312

[65] Carol P. Christ, *Rebirth of the Goddess,* (Routledge, NY, 1997) p. 66

[66] Also see p. 22, *Our Mother and Father God,* (Bookstand Publishing, CA, 2014)

[67] Joy F. Reichard, *Celebrate the Divine Feminine*, (Bush St. Press, CA, 2011) p. 38

[68] Alan Butler, City of the Goddess, (Watkins Publishing, UK, 2011) p. 25

[69] Barbara G. Walker, *Restoring the Goddess: Equal Rights for Modern Women* (Amherst, NY: Prometheus Books, 2000), p. 33

[70] Barbara G. Walker, *Restoring the Goddess: Equal Rights for Modern Women* (Amherst, NY: Prometheus Books, 2000), p. 37

[71] Elaine Pagels, *The Gnostic Gospels,* (Vintage Books, NY, 1989) p. 57

[72] Anne Baring, *The Myth of the Goddess,* (Penguin Group, NY, 1991) p. 461

[73] Merlin Stone, *When God Was a Woman,* (Harcourt, FL, 1976) p. 240

[74] Rev. Dr. Karen Tate, *Voices of the Sacred Feminine*, (Changemakers Books, UK, 2014) p. 90

[75] Barbara G. Walker, *Restoring the Goddess: Equal Rights for Modern Women* (Amherst, NY: Prometheus Books, 2000), p. 35

[76] Sylvia Browne, *God, Creation, and Tools for Life*, (Hay House, CA, 2000) p. 25

[77] Anne Baring, *The Myth of the Goddess*, (Penguin Group, NY, 1991) p. 611

[78] Carol Schaefer, *Grandmothers Counsel the World*, (Trumpeter Books, MA, 2006) p. 134

[79] Alix Pirani, *The Absent Mother*, (Mandala, London, 1991) p. 132

[80] Barbara G. Walker, *Restoring the Goddess*, (Prometheus Books, NY, 2000) p. 81

[81] Carol Schaefer, *Grandmothers Counsel the World*, (Trumpeter Books, MA, 2006) p. 102

[82] Also see p. 18, *Our Mother and Father God*, (Bookstand Publishing, CA, 2014)

[83] Carol Schaefer, *Grandmothers Counsel the World*, (Trumpeter Books, MA, 2006) p. 133

[84] Anne Baring, *The Myth of the Goddess*, (Penguin Books, NY, 1991) p. xii

[85] Alix Pirani, *The Absent Mother*, (Mandala, London, 1991) p. 129

[86] Elizabeth A. Johnson, *She Who Is*, (Crossroad Publishing, New York, 1986) p. 15

[87] Also see p. 8, *Who Is Mother God?* (Outskirts Press, CO, 2014)

[88] Carol P. Christ, *Rebirth of the Goddess*, (Routledge, NY, 1997) p. 23

Chapter 3 What Will Happen When She Reappears?

[89] Janet Wolter and Alan Butler, *America, Nation of the Goddess*, Destiny Books, VT. 2015 p.12

[90] Karen Speestra, *Sophia, The Feminine Face of God*, (Michael Weise Productions, CA) p. xx

[91] Nancy Oakes, *Return of Sophia*, (CreateSpace, SC, 2013) p. 69

[92] Caitlin Matthews, *Sophia*, (Quest Books, IL, 2009) p. 42

[93] Karen Speestra, *Sophia, The Feminine Face of God*, (Michael Weise Prod., CA, 2011) p. xix

[94] Sylvia Browne, *God, Creation, and Tools for Life*, (Hay House, CA, 2000) p. 55

[95] Rev. Jann Aldredge-Clanton, *She Lives*, (Skylight Paths Publishing, VT, 2014) p. 200

[96] Robert Powell and Estelle Isaacson, *The Mystery of Sophia*, (Lindisfarne Books, MA, 2014) p. 128

[97] Robert Powell and Estelle Isaacson, *The Mystery of Sophia*, (Lindisfarne Books, MA, 2014) p. 147

[98] Susan Cady, *Wisdom's Feast*, (Harper & Row, NY, 1986) p. 62

[99] Sylvia Browne, *God, Creation, and Tools for Life*, (Hay House, CA, 2000) p. 66

[100] Anne Baring, *The Myth of the Goddess*, (Penguin Group, NY, 1991) p. xi

[101] Vajra Ma, *From a Hidden Stream*, (Vajra Ma, 2013) p. 17

[102] Carol Schaefer, *Grandmothers Counsel the World*, (Trumpeter Books, MA, 2006) p. 134

[103] Nancy Oakes, *Return of Sophia*, (CreateSpace, SC, 2013) p. 23

[104] Robert Powell, *The Sophia Teachings*, (Lindisfarne Books, MA, 2011) p. 2

[105] Carol P. Christ, *Rebirth of the Goddess*, (Routledge, NY, 1997) p. 121

[106] Andrew Harvey, *The Return of the Mother*, (Frog Ltd, CA, 1995) p. 37

[107] See also p. 23, *Our Mother and Father God*, (Bookstand Publishing, CA, 2014)

[108] See also p. 21, *Our Mother and Father God*, (Bookstand Publishing, CA, 2014)

[109] Robert Powell and Estelle Isaacson, *The Mystery of Sophia*, (Lindisfarne Books, MA, 2014) p. 145

[110] Carol P. Christ, *Rebirth of the Goddess*, (Routledge, NY, 1997) p. xii

[111] Nancy Oakes, *Return of Sophia*, (CreateSpace, SC, 2013) p. xii

[112] Asphodel P. Long, *In a Chariot Drawn by Lions*, (Crossing Press, CA, 1993) p. 60

[113] Tricia McCannon, *Return of the Divine Sophia*, (Bear & Co., VT, 2015) p. 167

[114] Rev. Dr. Karen Tate, *Voices of the Sacred Feminine*, (Changemakers Books, UK, 2014) p. 133

[115] Carol P. Christ, *Rebirth of the Goddess*, (Routledge, NY, 1997) p. 46

[116] See also p. 13, *Our Mother and Father God*, (Bookstand Publishing, CA, 2014)

Chapter 4 How Do I Relate to Mother God?

[117] See also p. 14, *Our Mother and Father God*, (Bookstand Publishing, CA, 2014)

[118] Susan Cady, *Wisdom's Feast*, (Harper & Row, NY, 1986) p. 64

[119] See also p. 15, *Our Mother and Father God*, (Bookstand Publishing, CA, 2014)

[120] Asphodel P. Long, *In a Chariot Drawn by Lions*, (Crossing Press, CA, 1993) p. 44

[121] Tim Bulkeley, *Not Only a Father*, (Archer Press, New Zealand, 2011) p. 6

[122] Asphodel P. Long, *In a Chariot Drawn by Lions*, (Crossing Press, CA, 1993) p. 56

[123] Jennifer Barker Woolger, *The Goddess Within*, (Ballantine Books, NY, 1989) p. 15

[124] Sondra Ray, *Rock Your World with the Divine Mother*, (New World Library, CA, 2007) p. xiii

[125] Susan Cady, *Wisdom's Feast*, (Harper & Row, NY, 1986) p. 62

[126] William Bond and Pamela Suffield, Gospel of the Goddess, (Artemis Creation Publishing, NY 1989) p. 156

[127] Alix Pirani, *The Absent Mother*, (Mandala, London, 1991) p. 108

[128] Andrew Harvey, *The Return of the Mother*, (Frog Ltd, CA, 1995) p. 125

[129] Andrew Harvey, *The Return of the Mother*, (Frog Ltd, CA, 1995) p. 207

[130] Andrew Harvey, *The Return of the Mother*, (Frog Ltd, CA, 1995) p. 107

[131] William Bond and Pamela Suffield, *Gospel of the Goddess*, (Artemis Creation Publishing, NY, 1989) p. 150

[132] William Bond and Pamela Suffield, *Gospel of the Goddess*,

(Artemis Creation Publishing, NY, 1989) p. 149

[133] Andrew Harvey, *The Return of the Mother,* (Frog Ltd, CA, 1995) p. 164

[134] Paul R. Smith, *Is it Okay to Call God "Mother",* (Hendrickson Press, MA, 1993) p. 170

[135] Asphodel P. Long, *In a Chariot Drawn by Lions,* (Crossing Press, CA, 1993) p. 94

[136] Robert Powell and Estelle Isaacson, *The Mystery of Sophia,* (Lindisfarne Books, MA, 2014) p. 139

[137] Caitlin Matthews, *Sophia,* (Quest Books, IL, 2009) p. 324

[138] Rev. Dr. Karen Tate, *Voices of the Sacred Feminine,* (Changemakers Books, UK, 2014) p. 15

Chapter 5 Mother God: Parent and Role Model for Women

[139] Cathy Pagano, *Wisdom's Daughters,* (Balboa Press, IN, 2013) p. 214

[140] Sylvia Browne, *God, Creation, and Tools for Life,* (Hay House, CA, 2000) p. 15

[141] Tricia McCannon, *Return of the Divine Sophia,* (Bear & Co., VT, 2015) p. 316

[142] Tricia McCannon, *Return of the Divine Sophia,* (Bear & Co., VT, 2015) p. 322

[143] Tricia McCannon, *Return of the Divine Sophia,* (Bear & Co., VT, 2015) p. 349

[144] Alan Butler, *City of the Goddess,* (Watkins Publishing, UK, 2011) p. xv

[145] L. Juliana M. Claassens, *Mourner, Mother, Midwife,* (Westminister John Knox, KY, 2012) p. 24

[146] L. Juliana M. Claassens, *Mourner, Mother, Midwife,* (Westminister John Knox, KY, 2012) p. 33

[147] L. Juliana M. Claassens, *Mourner, Mother, Midwife,* (Westminister John Knox, KY, 2012) p. 35

[148] Vajra Ma, *From a Hidden Stream,* (Vajra Ma, 2013) p. 31

[149] Jennifer Barker Woolger, *The Goddess Within,* (Ballantine Books, NY, 1989) p. 26

[150] William Bond and Pamela Suffield, *Gospel of the Goddess,*

(Artemis Creation Publishing, NY, 1989) p. 166

[151] William Bond and Pamela Suffield, *Gospel of the Goddess,* (Artemis Creation Publishing, NY, 1989) p. 15

[152] William Bond and Pamela Suffield, *Gospel of the Goddess,* (Artemis Creation Publishing, NY, 1989) 165

[153] See also p. 5, *Our Mother and Father God,* (Bookstand Publishing, CA, 2014)

[154] https://www.inclusivesecurity.org/publication/why-women-inclusive-security-and-peaceful-societies/

[155] See also p. 8, *Our Mother and Father God,* (Bookstand Publishing, CA, 2014)

[156] Carol Ochs, *Behind the Sex of God,* (Beacon Press, MA, 1977) p. 120

[157] See also p. 14, *Our Mother and Father God,* (Bookstand Publishing, CA, 2014)

[158] Harvey, Andrew, *The Divine Feminine,* (Conari Press, CA, 1996) p. 88

[159] Rev. Jann Aldredge-Clanton, *She Lives,* (Skylight Paths Publishing, VT, 2014) 216

Chapter 6 Testimonies About Mother God

[160] Sondra Ray, *Rock Your World with the Divine Mother,* (New World Library, CA, 2007) p. 30

[161] Sri Aurobindo, *The Mother,* (Lotus Press, WI, 1995) p. 52

[162] Andrew Harvey, *The Return of the Mother,* (Frog Ltd, CA, 1995) p. 32

[163] Robert Powell, *The Sophia Teachings,* (Lindisfarne Books, MA, 2011) p. 136

[164] William Bond and Pamela Suffield, *Gospel of the Goddess,* (Artemis Creation Publishing, NY, 1989) p. 16

[165] Sondra Ray, *Rock Your World with the Divine Mother,* (New World Library, CA, 2007) p. 77

[166] Sri Aurobindo, *The Mother,* (Lotus Press, WI, 1995) p. 43

[167] Rev. Dr. Karen Tate, *Voices of the Sacred Feminine,* (Changemakers Books, UK, 2014) p. 86

[168] Joan Chamberlain Engelsman, *The Feminine Dimension of the Divine,* (Westminister Press, PA, 1979) p. 23

[169] Shirley Nicholson, *The Goddess Reawakening,* (Quest Books, IL, 1992) p. 216

[170] Sondra Ray, *Rock Your World with the Divine Mother,* (New World Library, CA, 2007) p. xii

[171] Andrew Harvey, *The Return of the Mother,* (Frog Ltd, CA, 1995) p. 81

[172] Jennifer Barker Woolger, *The Goddess Within*, (Ballantine Books, NY, 1989) p. 258

[173] Cathy Pagano, *Wisdom's Daughters,* (Balboa Press, IN, 2013) p. 214

[174] Robert Powell and Estelle Isaacson, *The Mystery of Sophia* (Lindisfarne Books, MA, 2014) p. 11

[175] Caitlin Matthews, *Sophia,* (Quest Books, IL, 2009) p. 350

[176] Barbara G. Walker, *Restoring the Goddess, Equal Rights for Modern Women* (Amherst, NY: Prometheus Books, 2000) p. 42

[177] Andrew Harvey, *The Return of the Mother,* (Frog Ltd, CA, 1995) p. 204

[178] Carol P. Christ, *Rebirth of the Goddess,* (Routledge, NY, 1997) p. 55

[179] Monica Sjoo and Barbara Mor, *The Great Cosmic Mother,* (Harper, NY, 1987) p. 420

[180] Carol Schaefer, *Grandmothers Counsel the World*, (Trumpeter Books, MA, 2006) p. 115

[181] Hallie Iglehart Austen, *The Heart of the Goddess*, (Wingbow Press, CA, 1990) p. xv

[182] Teri Degler, *The Divine Feminine Fire,* (Dreamriver Press, PA, 2009) p. 89

[183] Shirley Nicholson, *The Goddess Reawakening,* (Quest Books, IL, 1992) p. 68

[184] Tricia McCannon, *Return of the Divine Sophia,* (Bear & Co., VT, 2015) p. 320

[185] Robert Powell and Estelle Isaacson, *The Mystery of Sophia,* (Lindisfarne Books, MA, 2014) p. 47

[186] Asphodel P. Long, *In a Chariot Drawn by Lions,* (Crossing Press, CA, 1993) p. 48

[187] Andrew Harvey, *The Return of the Mother,* (Frog Ltd, CA, 1995) p. 118

[188] Sri Aurobindo, *The Mother,* (Lotus Press, WI, 1995) p. 38

[189] Nancy Oakes, *Return of Sophia*, (CreateSpace, SC, 2013) p. 33

[190] Robert Powell and Estelle Isaacson, *The Mystery of Sophia,* (Lindisfarne Books, MA, 2014) p. 42

[191] Asphodel P. Long, *In a Chariot Drawn by Lions,* (Crossing Press, CA, 1993) p. 76

[192] Teri Degler, *The Divine Feminine Fire,* (Dreamriver Press, PA, 2009) p. 141

[193] Robert Powell, *The Sophia Teachings,* (Lindisfarne Books, MA, 2011) p. 15

[194] Karen Speestra, *Sophia, The Feminine Face of God,* (Michael Weise Prod., CA, 2011) p. 151

[195] Caitlin Matthews, *Sophia,* (Quest Books, IL, 2009) p. xxv

[196] Robert Powell and Estelle Isaacson, *The Mystery of Sophia,* (Lindisfarne Books, MA, 2014) p. x

[197] Elizabeth A. Johnson *She Who Is*, (Crossroad Publishing, NY, 1996) p. 135

[198] Karen Speestra, *Sophia, The Feminine Face of God,* (Michael Weise Prod. CA, 2011) p. 306

[199] Tricia McCannon, *Return of the Divine Sophia,* (Bear & Co., VT, 2015) p. 22

[200] Rev. Dr. Karen Tate, *Voices of the Sacred Feminine,* (Changemakers Books, UK, 2014) p. 91

[201] Urantia Book 38:1.3 (418.6)

[202] Nancy Oakes, *Return of Sophia*, (CreateSpace, SC, 2013) p. 46

[203] Robert Powell and Estelle Isaacson, *The Mystery of Sophia,* (Lindisfarne Books, MA, 2014) p. 41

[204] Monica Sjoo and Barbara Mor, *The Great Cosmic Mother,* (Harper, NY, 1987) p. xviii

[205] Elizabeth A. Johnson *She Who Is*, (Crossroad Publishing, NY, 1996) p. 136

[206] Robert Powell and Estelle Isaacson, *The Mystery of Sophia,* (Lindisfarne Books, MA, 2014) p. 134

[207] Sondra Ray, *Rock Your World with the Divine Mother,* (New World Library, CA, 2007) p. 199

[208] Bible's *New Testament*, Revelation 12:1

[209] Barbara G. Walker, *Restoring the Goddess: Equal Rights for Modern Women* (Amherst, NY: Prometheus Books, 2000), p. 222

[210] Hallie Iglehart Austen, *The Heart of the Goddess*, (Wingbow Press, CA, 1990) p. xxiii

[211] Paul R. Smith, *Is it Okay to Call God "Mother"*, (Hendrickson Press, MA, 1993) p. 191

[212] Margot Adler, *Drawing Down the Moon*, (Penguin Books, New York, 1986) p. 205

[213] Sylvia Browne, *Mother God*, (Hay House, CA, 2004) p. 76

[214] Susanne Schaup, *Sophia, Aspects of the Divine Feminine*, (Nicholas-Hays, ME, 1997) p. 174

[215] Sylvia Browne, *Mother God*, (Hay House, CA, 2004) p. 95

[216] Thomas Schipflinger, *Sophia-Maria*, (Samuel Weiser, ME, 1998) p. 221

[217] Barbara G. Walker, *Restoring the Goddess, Equal Rights for Modern Women* (Amherst, NY: Prometheus Books, 2000), p. 221

[218] Carol P. Christ, *Rebirth of the Goddess*, (Routledge, NY, 1997) p. 28

[219] Ron Pappalardo, *Reconciled by the Light, Book II*, (CreateSpace, 2013) p. 83

Chapter 7 In Her Own Words

[220] Mare Cromwell, *The Great Mother Bible*, (Pamoon Press, MD, 2014) pp. 26-27

[221] Merlin Stone, *When God Was a Woman*, (Harcourt, FL, 1976) p. 22

[222] Dorothy Atalla, *Conversations with the Goddess*, (Pharos Press, WI, 2010) p. 257

[223] Andrew Harvey, *The Return of the Mother*, (Frog Ltd, CA, 1995) p. 439

[224] Tricia McCannon, *Return of the Divine Sophia*, (Bear & Co., VT, 2015) p. 37

[225] Robert Powell and Estelle Isaacson, *The Mystery of Sophia*, (Lindisfarne Books, MA, 2014) p. 34

[226] Robert Powell and Estelle Isaacson, *The Mystery of Sophia*, (Lindisfarne Books, MA, 2014) p. 32

[227] Dorothy Atalla, *Conversations with the Goddess*, (Pharos Press, WI, 2010) p. 107

[228] Mare Cromwell, *The Great Mother Bible*, (Pamoon Press, MD, 2014) pp. 98-99

[229] Robert Powell, *The Sophia Teachings*, (Lindisfarne Books, MA, 2011) p. 135

[230] Andrew Harvey, *The Return of the Mother*, (Frog Ltd, CA, 1995) p. 126

Chapter 11 The Search for Peace

[231] Paul R. Smith, *Is it Okay to Call God "Mother"?* (Hendrickson Press, MA, 1993) p. 213

[232] Robert Powell, *The Sophia Teachings*, (Lindisfarne Books, MA, 2011) p. 129

[233] http://www.mothergod.info/new-messages (Oct. 18, 2015)

[234] Andrew Harvey, *The Return of the Mother*, (Frog Ltd, CA, 1995) p. 112

[235] Rev. Dr. Karen Tate, *Voices of the Sacred Feminine*, (Changemakers Books, UK, 2014) p. 9

[236] Tricia McCannon, *Return of the Divine Sophia*, (Bear & Co., VT, 2015) p. 143

[237] Dorothy Atalla, *Conversations with the Goddess*, (Pharos Press, WI, 2010) p. 42

[238] Nancy Oakes, *Return of Sophia*, (CreateSpace, SC, 2013) p. 71

[239] J. Lyn Studebaker, *Switching to Goddess*, (O Books, UK, 2008) p. 288

[240] William Bond and Pamela Suffield, *Gospel of the Goddess*, (Artemis Creation Publishing, NY, 1989) p. 23

[241] Frances Beer, *Julian of Norwich*, (D.S. Brewer, Cambridge, 1998) p. 63

[242] William Bond and Pamela Suffield, *Gospel of the Goddess*, (Artemis Creation Publishing, NY, 1989) p. 34

[243] William Bond and Pamela Suffield, *Gospel of the Goddess*, (Artemis Creation Publishing, NY, 1989) p. 29

[244] Dorothy Atalla, *Conversations with the Goddess,* (Pharos Press, WI, 2010) p. 107

[245] Rosemary Radford Ruether, *Goddesses and the Divine Feminine*, (Univ. of CA. Press, CA, 2005) p. 276

[246] Carol P. Christ, *Rebirth of the Goddess,* (Routledge, NY, 1997) p. 91

[247] Tim Bulkeley, *Not Only a Father*, (Archer Press, New Zealand, 2011) p. 120

[248] Virginia Ramey Mollenkott, *The Divine Feminine, the Biblical Imagery of God as Female*, (Crossroad Publishing, NY, 1989) p. 116

[249] Tricia McCannon, *Return of the Divine Sophia,* (Bear & Co., VT, 2015) p. 407

[250] Jennifer Barker Woolger, *The Goddess Within*, (Ballantine Books, NY, 1989) p. 17

[251] William Bond and Pamela Suffield, *Gospel of the Goddess,* (Artemis Creation Publishing, NY, 1989) p. 143

[252] Jennifer Barker Woolger, *The Goddess Within*, (Ballantine Books, NY, 1989) p. 404

[253] Harvey, Andrew, *The Divine Feminine*, (Conari Press, CA, 1996) p. 182

[254] Robert Powell and Estelle Isaacson, *The Mystery of Sophia,* (Lindisfarne Books, MA, 2014) p. 20

[255] Harvey, Andrew, *The Divine Feminine*, (Conari Press, CA, 1996) p. 13

[256] Nancy Oakes, *Return of Sophia*, (CreateSpace, SC, 2013) p. 72

Conclusion

[257] Dorothy Atalla, *Conversations with the Goddess,* (Pharos Press, WI, 2010) p. 275

[258] See also p. 103, *Who Is Mother God?* (Outskirts Press, CO, 2014)

[259] J. Lyn Studebaker, *Switching to Goddess*, (O Books, UK, 2008) p. 268

[260] Elizabeth A. Johnson *She Who Is*, (Crossroad Publishing, NY, 1996) p. 180

[261] Lynn Rogers, *Edgar Cayce and the Eternal Feminine,* (We Publish Books, IL, 1993) p. 97

[262] Tim Bulkeley, *Not Only a Father,* (Archer Press, New Zealand, 2011) p. 121

[263] Vajra Ma, *From a Hidden Stream,* (Vajra Ma, 2013) p. 24

[264] Vajra Ma, *From a Hidden Stream,* (Vajra Ma, 2013) p. 24

[265] Paul R. Smith, *Is it Okay to Call God "Mother"?* (Hendrickson Press, MA, 1993) p. 273

[266] Carol Schaefer, *Grandmothers Counsel the World,* (Trumpeter Books, MA, 2006) p. 122

[267] Vajra Ma, *From a Hidden Stream,* (Vajra Ma, 2013) p. 67

67473510R00100

Made in the USA
Charleston, SC
13 February 2017